D1568185

Critical Assembly

Mary Burritt Christiansen Poetry Series

The Mary Burritt Christiansen Poetry Series publishes
two to four books a year that engage and give voice to
the realities of living, working, and experiencing the
West and the Border as places and as metaphors. The
purpose of the series is to expand access to, and the
audience for, quality poetry, both single volumes and
anthologies, that can be used for general reading as
well as in classrooms.

Mary Burritt
Christiansen
Poetry Series

Also available in the Mary Burritt Christiansen Poetry Series:

Ground, Wind, This Body: Poems by Tina Carlson
MEAN/TIME: Poems by Grace Bauer
América invertida: An Anthology of Emerging Uruguayan Poets
edited by Jesse Lee Kercheval
Untrussed: Poems by Christine Stewart-Nuñez
Family Resemblances: Poems by Carrie Shipers
The Woman Who Married a Bear: Poems by Tiffany Midge
Self-Portrait with Spurs and Sulfur: Poems by Casey Thayer
Crossing Over: Poems by Priscilla Long
Heresies: Poems by Orlando Ricardo Menes
Report to the Department of the Interior: Poems by Diane Glancy

For additional titles in the Mary Burritt Christiansen Poetry Series,
please visit unmpress.com.

Critical Assembly

Poems of the Manhattan Project

John Canaday

University of New Mexico Press • Albuquerque

Library of Congress Cataloging-in-Publication Data
Names: Canaday, John, 1961– author.
Title: Critical Assembly: Poems of the Manhattan Project / John Canaday.
Description: Albuquerque: University of New Mexico Press, 2017. | Series: Mary Burritt
    Christiansen Poetry Series | Includes bibliographical references. |
Identifiers: LCCN 2017011130 (print) | LCCN 2017028534 (ebook) | ISBN 9780826358837
    (paperback) | ISBN 9780826358844 (E-book)
Subjects: LCSH: Manhattan Project (U.S.)—Poetry. | Atomic bomb—Poetry. | Nuclear
    physicists—Poetry. | Nuclear energy—Poetry. | BISAC: POETRY / General.
Classification: LCC PS3603.A524 (ebook) | LCC PS3603.A524 C75 2017 (print) | DDC 811/.6—
    dc23
LC record available at https://lccn.loc.gov/2017011130

Cover photographs courtesy of Los Alamos National Labratory
Cover designed by Felicia Cedillos
Composed in Dante Mt Std 10.5/15

for Sami

The true men of action in our time, those who transform the world, are not the politicians and statesmen, but the scientists. Unfortunately, poetry cannot celebrate them because their deeds are concerned with things, not persons, and are, therefore, speechless.

—W. H. AUDEN

Biologically, physiologically, we are not so different from each other; historically, as narratives—we are each of us unique.

—OLIVER SACKS

Contents

ΔH / HEAT

Medialog: William Laurence

Reporter, New York Times

At Trinity, little men birthed a great solar burst: light
a billion years chained in Earth's bones. Alien. A cursed light.

Zero their minds and Zero hearts. They knew no time, no space
except of their design. All day, lab bound, they coerced light.

Longing to repeat God's opening salvo, "Let there be . . . ,"
they roughed out doomsday. Forged a final echo of first light.

The desert melted. Rabbits, badgers roasted miles away.
Success that could be seen only in the best (or worst) light.

The longhairs worshipped the great god It of the occasion.
They danced like primitives around their fire's thirsty light.

When Farrell blurted, "Now the war is over," Groves scoffed, "Sure.
Once our sun has risen on Japan"—his tone perverse, light.

A bystander with a byline, when I got underfoot
they called me "Writer's Block." While I doctored words, they nursed light.

U

Albert Einstein

Faculty, Institute for Advanced Study

Life is finite
               and improbable.
My prow points out across Peconic Bay.
The tiller, worn as smooth as living skin,

trembles under my fingers' wooden grip.
What was the chance of my appearing here
and now? And yet my sail has only filled

as nature willed, and as its laws decree
the water, white capped, wrestles with the wind.
I wrestle both, though each of us obeys

and manifests the selfsame laws.
The instruments are mortal, what we measure
infinite. Mankind's proper posture

must be awe: our bodies' currents carry us,
like Newton (grant we travel half so far),
toward revelation of the limits God

has set on nature. Are we fit to know
such secrets? We cannot resist the sweet
temptation of the possible: we eat

the apple, build machineries of war,
reshape the world in our short-sighted image;
yet no physicist could have a soul so poor

he would not do as much to see God's face.
Nostra culpa! The more we know, the less
we feel. Man cools more quickly than the earth.

Leo Szilard

Physicist

In 1913, H. G. Wells produced *The World
Set Free*. It's fiction, yes, and Wells a dilettante,
no doubt—his books chock full of wild imaginings.
He does his homework, though, learns physics, chemistry,
and through some kind of alchemy or calculus,
divines the ends of other men's discoveries.
But still: Atomic bombs? A global war? Moonshine,
as Rutherford would say—with all the Cavendish
to echo him.
                    And I agreed. Too earnestly.
I knew reality from make-believe—knew Wells,
a little—saw him throw a fork across the room
in Otto Mandl's London flat. The public mask
he'd fashioned, hating masks, had trapped him in such shows
of studied spontaneity. Yet he is fierce
in his pursuit of truth. He cares more for ideas
than men—and so he dedicates *The World Set Free*
to Frederick Soddy's book on radium and not
its author. Individuals will come and go,
but what we think and write lives on to bless or haunt
the future. Wells's work is the haunting sort.

My colleagues fancy we are experts. I disdain
the name. Most experts focus on what can't be done.
A dogged dabbler, Wells predicted man-
made radioactivity in '33—
he named the very year! And now that fiction's proved
a fact, the rest seems . . . plausible. And so I sip
Wells's moonshine. Lounging in the hotel tub past noon,
like Archimedes dreaming Hiero's crown, I bribe
my body with a long, hot bath and let my mind

float free—until the maid descends in thunder, casts
me out to wander London, wondering. I stroll
along Southampton Row. A red light breaks my chain
of thought. I balance on the curb, the light turns green,
and then a swift, sweet surge of inspiration hits:
the missing piece must be a massive element
that will absorb a single neutron, hold it briefly,
then emit two more: a self-sustaining chain
reaction! Passersby are spared a naked roar,
"Eureka!" since I have no tub to leap from. Grumps,
they frown on dancing.
                                        Only slowly does the joy
of insight give way to a more foreboding thought.
I cannot publish this. Then what? Develop it?
Or take a patent on the Admiralty's behalf
and pray that no one in the Reich reads H. G. Wells?
But if all knowledge comes through individuals,
it comes to answer questions asked by history.
I know that one day soon I'll have to make a choice,
or sit back in my bath and have it made for me.

Eugene Wigner

Physicist

Hatred's homicidal.
Hitler knows. He makes
what most men mean by hate
a tepid sentiment. And still
the Jews refuse to rouse
themselves. O when
will my Hungarians
awaken? Only slowly
are they moved to anger;
even then most merely say,
"Depose the madman."
Moderation's suicide.
A whimper while the butcher
spreads fresh paper.
Even in translation
in the *Times*, he aims
his hate at me, my family
trapped in Budapest.
Our decades-old conversion's
meaningless. In Nazi law,
I could become a *hausfrau*
more easily than Lutheran.
Why should I hesitate
to bend my skills to fight?
Yes, even kill.
My Princeton colleagues
wince. I challenge them
to say which wrong
they disapprove of more:
the braying Nazi donkeys,
or this sometime Jew
who has the questionable taste
to corner them.

Otto Frisch

Physicist

Chancellors come and go. So
      when Hitler called
my darling *Kernphysik*
      a Jewish trick,
I mocked his ignorance,
      too blind to worry
till our lab was stamped
      zu jüdisch. Shamed,
Stern shilled my resume
      abroad, sold me
to Blackett, cheap. I thanked him,
      only thinking,
Leave this filthy place!
      while Aryan friends
declared in wistful tones,
      "You're fortunate:
no need to feel complicit."
      As though my smile
were not a compromise.
      As though forgiving
such parting Judas kisses
      might grant me grace.

Hope builds nests in strange places.
      Aunt Lise stayed.
Austrian, she eschewed
      her Jewish roots,
preferring to lose herself
      in Nature's mists.
She clung to hard-won words:
      Acting Institute
Director. But then the *Anschluss*

scythed her mooring.
Stateless, suddenly,
  forced to confess
a false embarrassment—
  impure descent—
she fled, left isotopes
  of radium
(she thought) still on her desk.
  God Himself
only barely saved her.
  But what of Dad
interned in Dachau, Mum
  stunned, grieving
in Vienna, unbelieving
  higher powers
willing to intervene?
  Stubborn, stricken,
I stick to physics, as though
  it might somehow
confirm my blinkered faith
  for once and make
his passport come. As though
  despite men's malice,
and great as God may be,
  physics is bigger.

Max Delbrück

Geneticist; former physicist

Niels Bohr was God. We added up
the letters of his least remark—
and if he mumbled, if we quibbled
with how he harped on classical
space-time irrationality,
we knew he spoke for Nature
like no one else alive—at least
since Einstein left the quantum world
to follow, as it seemed, the muse
that once had whispered in his ear,
"E equals M times C quadrat."
Was Herr Professor Einstein privy
to what we commoners were not?
No doubt. But was he right to say
that physicists had been bewitched
by mere statistical success?
My classmates thought him past his prime.
I couldn't say. A world in shambles
greeted me each morning: thuggish
Brownshirts cheered by neighbors, friends;
the long depression deepening,
clogging our hearts. Even physics,
that Eden of the intellect,
seemed tainted by our discontent.
Layer after layer intervened
between our senses and the objects
we observed, until the facts
themselves defeated common sense.
We entertained the wildest theories
hoping to resolve confusions
our efforts only added to.
New particles appeared like moths.

Which should we believe in? Neutrons,
lacking charge but tangible,
pinned in the lab by Chadwick's gaze?
Neutrinos, massless, fluttering
in the flame of Pauli's intellect?
If Heisenberg and Schrödinger
were stopgaps, who deserved our faith?
Bohr's benediction might erase
a fraction of the doubt we felt—
although his gentle, dreaded "Not
to criticize your theory, but,"
was likelier. If metaphors
for subatomic processes
were hard to come by—or too easy—
how could we describe the chaos
going on inside us? I tried
with little luck. Then there it was:
a parallel both apropos
and inescapable. The man
who hasn't sometimes felt, like Faust,
a sense of his own emptiness
in the presence of a pretty girl,
Allegri's *Miserere*, Chartres
Cathedral, or the Calculus
might just as well be dead. Lust drives
achievement. What I wouldn't give
to lose myself in something greater
is myself. The devil is
dissatisfaction. Longing. Need.
He sent us packing every spring
to join Bohr's Copenhagen cadre
for a conference on the current hash
of theory and experiment.
Young, avid, brash, uncertainty
took all our love. Unbearable.

And so we junior men devised
a stunt to parody the work
we all believed too strongly in,
with Bohr as God, and Ehrenfest
his Faust. He stood for all of us:
our drive for knowledge, influence,
prestige—the fruits that fed a life
lived in the mind. Dear Pauli, brusque
and irritable as ever, won
the role of Mephistopheles,
in which he tempted Ehrenfest
with *Strahlungstheorie*, $\Psi\Psi^\star$,
and infinite self-energy—
but most of all with Pauli's own
neutrino, which we'd tricked up as
a cardboard cutout Gretchen, voiced
by Ellen Tvede, Weisskopf's flame:
"Without me, Beta rays unfix,
N-spin's unspun, statistics stick."
Although the tone was light, we felt
a real despair at the unholy
hurly-burly of the discipline.
We courted laughter and applause,
while each of us, in truth, aspired
to Godhead—whether as Bohr's heir
or, hardly less immodestly,
as witness to the mysteries
on which the heavenly axles turn.
In the blizzard of hypotheses
that raged around us, some were bound
to be correct—or so we wagered.
With what currency? Our souls?
Our selves? Whichever way one says it,
the price was high. When Ehrenfest
gave in to the "DESPERATION"

many of us felt, and quit the game,
it should have signaled something wrong.
But few among us listened. Work
went on, relentless, building toward
a crisis we did not foresee.
I didn't see it, certainly.
Did Ehrenfest? I doubt it, though
his suicide saved me, at least.
It made me wonder, where was physics
taking us? I couldn't answer.
So I resolved to give it up.
I learned biology and spent
my days deciphering the lives
of cells seduced by viruses.
Not to criticize my colleagues!
They didn't know where it would lead.
If anyone had asked, I'm sure
they would have said, God only knows.

Otto Frisch

Physicist

Rare earth sparks the clouds
　　　between two wars.
Fermi, Hahn and Strassmann,
　　　Joliot-Curie—
all physicists and chemists
　　　track protons now.
They're alchemists, like Newton:
　　　decay's their meat.
Too poor to feast, I scrounged
　　　for bits and bobs.
(I lined my chamber once
　　　with Woolworth's ladies'
plain black underwear.)
　　　Physics is best
played playfully, like love,
　　　a four-hand piece:
Grieg's *Valse Caprice*. Friends
　　　and a little lightning's
all one needs to follow
　　　greater men.

Come Christmas, Lise, lonely,
　　　summons me
north to Kungälv where
　　　we'll celebrate
past celebrations. Split,
　　　scattered, family
now means more than once
　　　before. Or less.
Otto's note arrests
　　　festivities.

The body's tagged at last.
       It's barium.
I strap on skis while Lise
       makes good her claim
to move as fast without.
       The woods that wall
the Göta älv become
       a conference room,
a fallen spruce's trunk
       our sticky seat.
I scribble on scraps of paper
       from my pockets' stock.
We know uranium
       can't crack in two
against the grain of Gamow's
       alpha theory.
Yet it does. We turn
       to Schrödinger
for insight—particles
       are waves. And Bohr:
a nucleus is liquid-
       like. Our thought:
that heavy nuclei
       must undulate
like jeweled meltwater strung
       on wind-tossed twigs.
In larger elements
       charge balances
the surface tension—even
       lightly struck
in capturing a neutron,
       the pseudo drop
will wobble, waist, and split.
       Physics lacks words

for what we think, its paths
        abstractions hacked
like quantum tunnels through
        nature's briar
patch, its packing fraction
        a thorn-knit thicket
where neutrons multiply
        like rabbits till . . .

The winter woods are gone.
        Our minds' meadows
bloom. We calculate
        the energy
released—two hundred
        MeV.
Greater men have known
        less luck. The worst
have seen to it. So how
        to publish this
since Hitler split our world?
        Nature and *Natur-*
wissenschaften—Frisch
        and Meitner, Hahn
and Strassmann. All our chamber
        groups disband.
The fragments fly, form new
        duets. Atoms
breed like cells. I name
        their splitting "fission,"
as if such parting could
        be understood
as something less like death.

Leo Szilard

Physicist

Not everyone can be as fortunate as Christ.
To sacrifice yourself and do some good takes luck.
I've had some luck and given one-fifth of my heart
to help the world. But always four-fifths I retained.
Perhaps it's right that I became a Calvinist:
there's something of the proselytizer in my soul,
and even Einstein heeds my call. And Wigner. And
his car. We set out from the King's Crown on the twelfth
to find the summer cottage of a Dr. Moore
where Einstein lives and sails and thinks his hermit's thoughts.
But Wigwam got us lost. Cutchogue and Scuttlehole,
Yaphank and Shirley Mastic proved enough to make
this pair of former Jews from Hungary despair.
The heat was deadly. No one knew the doctor or
his cottage. I had reached the end of my one-fifth.
But Wigwam parroted my words: "We have a duty."
No more, perhaps, than I deserved, and maybe less.
I asked a sunburned boy of seven if he knew
where Einstein lived. He pointed with his fishing rod,
"Of course I do." And so he did, for good or ill.
We sat with Herr Professor on a screened-in porch
and sipped iced tea. We spoke of my experiments,
the lattice of uranium and graphite, how
the neutrons multiplied, and he was quick to see
the danger: "Daran habe ich gar nicht gedacht."
I can't believe he hadn't thought of it before,
despite his self-sought exile for the past ten years.
Perhaps he wanted to believe it was not yet
a necessary fact. I shared that wish, of course,
though in my heart I knew the figures hadn't lied.
I feared we'd need Christ's luck before our work was done.

Albert Einstein

Faculty, Institute for Advanced Study

The Czechoslovak state is occupied,
the Nazis stockpile its uranium,
and Leo claims they plan to make a bomb.

He's had some crazier ideas. And if
I listened when he pitched induction flow
refrigerators, why not now? Perhaps

God has designed the world as I have thought,
and firing neutrons at the nuclei
of heavy atoms is like shooting birds

at night. But if I'm wrong, my data old?
It's not improbable that novel sources
of enormous energy exist. And if

we follow, then. . . . O grant us no such then!
If Leo's right, then all bombardments all
together since the first men used firearms

would be child's play to what we will unleash,
and we will build ourselves a future age
to make our coal-black present shine like gold.

Edward Teller

Physicist

Now Einstein knows me as Szilard's
chauffeur. I warm the stoop
while great men talk of physics, bombs.
Fame is a used Ford coupe.

One dreams of more. A mere adjunct,
I heard Einstein expound
God's mysteries. Even his *Punkts*
and *Kommas* were profound.

Later, at der Berliner Zoo,
the sweet spring sun fell mute.
Wigner inquired, made me confess
I felt a brainless brute.

"Yes, yes. We know stupidity's
a general human trait."
I sometimes wish his kind words true.
Then no one would be great.

A guest at Bohr's colloquium,
I sat beside him, awed,
and watched his face fall as I spoke
of Newton's physics' flaws.

He closed his eyes. Sat silently.
"You might as well," he murmured,
"say we aren't sitting, drinking tea,
but only dream your words."

Why strive for Truth? Humility
whispers a choice: take less
and add, mechanically, to top
what passes for success.

I tried that route. Great Heisenberg
assigned my doctoral work—
compute the H_2 ion's states—
as though I were a clerk.

The Thales groaned unmusically
in the students' common room,
despite the oil I wooed it with,
and physics lost its bloom.

But most when Heisenberg pranced through
complaining he had proved
the last great theorem: "Nothing left
that needs genius." I stewed.

And then resolved to prove him wrong.
In increments. Stumbling,
perhaps. But finding it. The next
big thing. The biggest thing.

Janet Coatesworth

Stenographer, Columbia University

I spent each August in the steno pool.
My girlfriends took vacations, called me crazy,
but with the faculty off to Cape May
and Long Island, it was an easy
buck. Only a few crackpots holed
up in their studies. Only the odd ones stayed.

When Marcie hooked her husband, it was April.
She drew a Law School dean, and with a bit of work
she landed him. This amazed
some of the girls. It didn't really bother
me: she'd hardly any looks to speak of,
and he lacked panache,
but in the spring, when soft salt breezes wash
the avenues and sunlight spills
from every window, you can fall in love
with anything, even the oddballs in New York.
Right or wrong, some days
we just look good to each other.

Who doesn't hope for such a day? Even half
expect it? I had to laugh
the breathless afternoon I pulled
a rumpled gnome you'd swear
had been rejected from a fairy tale. He insisted
I come to his room at the King's Crown where
he'd dictate "an important letter."
A girl can be fooled
only so many times. So what twisted
my arm, assuming I knew better?
Boredom and curiosity
are as good words as any.

Beside an unmade bed,
two battered tan suitcases
gaped. Discarded
clothes hung from a dozen places:
doorknobs, bedposts, chairs.
He closed the door too fast.
His guttural mutter
was soundtrack to a girl's worst fears:
"We mustn't be disturbed." I was. But then
before I found the strength to flee, he had undressed
a wingback. "Here.
Let us begin."

And so he did, hardly waiting
for me to sit. "To F. D. Roosevelt,
the White House." I almost felt
sorry for him, his apparent
belief his words would reach the president.
"The element uranium may yield
a new, important source of energy."
His sentences hung like strings
of colored beads he hoped would curtain off
the drab rooms of his life.
He nearly had my pity—
poor, sad bachelor mouse—
until I started wondering
how far his fantasies might go.
"Extremely powerful bombs of a new type may be
constructed." Did he wink then, baiting
me? Or was he hoping to impress a pretty
girl? Or was he dangerous?
I stopped him. Threw a window
open. Lit a Chesterfield.

I'd never squealed on an employer.

None had ever been this scary.
But I didn't trust my fear.
It felt like shorthand for a larger worry:
madmen taking over Europe, maybe. Here
was one of them, and threatening
the President. Or not. I'd make a lousy lawyer.
I didn't trust my own suspicions;
who else would? The cops? My boss? I'd sing
my song and end up losing my position.

A chorus of squabbling taxi horns
on Morningside. I flicked my cigarette
and closed the sash. My gnome had worn
a path around the bed,
and now he perched, impatient, on its worn duvet,
sweating like a newlywed.
I picked my pad and pencil up and sat.
"Germany has stopped the export of uranium.
That she should take such early action
might perhaps be understood . . ."
But not by me. I sought perfection
from ears to fingertips, to be a medium
unmoved by anything his muttering conveyed.
Until he closed, "Yours very truly, A. Einstein."
How asinine
men are! To think a woman could
be gotten by whatever he was getting at.
Or that I would forgive it and forget.

He was no Einstein, that's for certain.
I had his name right on my duty slip: Szilard.
But from that moment on I feigned
the ignorance he clearly hoped to find
in me—and called him "Dr. Lizard"
to his face. Harmless, probably,

and just my luck, I thought, as rain began to bead
on the windowpane like a curtain
drawn across the afternoon. An August shower:
you could feel the sun buried
behind the clouds, a veiled power
slowly burning free.

Albert Einstein

Faculty, Institute for Advanced Study

The grass is hazy in the humid air.
The lawn slopes toward the dock where *Tinef* waits.
Not yet. First, Helen says the mail has come.

She'll deal with most of it—the letters piled
beside her place at table. Only one
by mine. She left the blinds half drawn

against the heat, the way they were last week
when Leo's long sleeves soaked in slatted light.
I feel I'm breathing in a paper sack.

The wind out on the water will be fresh.
It's no decision, really. If a bomb
is possible, the Germans must not get it first.

And so we trust in the Americans.
Their Roosevelt is wise. But wise enough
to have and not to use? I doubt my strength,

knowing no curse of God, no plague, no rain
of sulfur could suffice as just revenge
upon the Nazis for their rancid crimes.

And then? Pandora's box stands open. All
the ills of nightmare stalk our waking lives.
We cannot buy or bully Nature's faith.

She does not whisper in our ears alone.
Once having learned her secrets, we will live
in fear of what she'll teach our enemies.

Perhaps it all will prove impossible.
I thought so once. In that case, well, thank God,
there'll be no guilt for having tried and failed.

To search for laws of nature is mankind's
most noble undertaking. Nothing can
eclipse the wonder or the joy I feel

to read a scientific article
that lifts the veil of nature with a hand
of subtlety and penetration both.

Pauli says the Unified Field Theory
is my hobbyhorse, and he's half right. The dock
creaks. *Tinef* rocks at tether. God's wake crests

on the horizon, though nearby it fades
to infinitesimal waves. My horse awaits.
I'll ride until I find

                    a finite sum.

E_K

E K

Alexander Sachs

Friend and advisor to Franklin Roosevelt

History's hard
        to write,
                harder
to revise.
        When Fulton told
            Napoleon,
"I can remove
        both wind and storm
            that guard your enemies,"
the Little Corporal
        glimpsed the world's
            new face
but left his steam fleet
        grounded
            in committee.
How best to best
        bit-a-bitarian
            bickering?
Even presidents
        are men;
            even geniuses
can't translate
        every mutant thought
            that might yield
great discoveries.
        I shall be
            your go-between,
dear Mr. President.
        (I've paid
            my way and

can't deduct it
          from my income tax,
                    so pay attention,
please.
          I'll be as brief
                    as history allows.)
No need to read
          Professor Einstein's
                    own words now:
we're all punch drunk
          on printer's ink,
                    and type's mascara
dripped in eyes.
          I'll summarize:
                    Experiments reveal
uranium
          is split by
                    and emits
neutrons.
          Three probabilities
                    arise:
Energy.
          Radiation.
                    Bombs.
(The last
          of unenvisaged
                    potency and scope.)
These United States
          are fortunately poised
                    to draw time drafts
on history's
          Bank & Trust.
                    Eager to serve
the nation that affords us
          hospitality,
                    these scholar-refugees

and I advise:

      now's the time:

            revise Neutrality:

transduce

      mere verbiage

            to action:

make scientists

      and soldiers

            talk.

.

Leslie Groves

Colonel, Army Corps of Engineers

Oh, that thing.
               Eleven years among
the soft-palmed momma's boys in Washington:
I've earned command of combat troops. I built
munitions plants and relocation camps,
the Pentagon—now nearly done. Those hacks
can go to heck before I let them axe
my chance to join the war and find some peace.

"But wouldn't Grace object?" Civilians. Most
a waste of God's good air. My Buddha knows
the sacrifices we must make. Her health
excused her, but she never used it, not
a single time. An army wife knows better.
Boo knows best of all. She runs a home
the way I run my office: jobs get done
or else she'll know the reason why. Weekends
she volunteers downtown or chaperones
the soldiers' dances at the base canteen.
She did me proud when Mrs. Roosevelt
invited us to tea.
               My work was vital—
war saw to that—and no one in the Corps
more qualified. I had to up the odds
that Somervell would let me off the hook.
I cornered him outside his office. (Catch
a busy man midstride, and to be free
he'll grant your wish as quick as any genie.)
But darn it, someone got to Somervell
before me, and he wouldn't touch my transfer.
He crossed his arms against his brass and said,
"You do this right, and it will win the war."

We both knew better, but he played it straight.
"Styer will fill you in." He'd earned his stripes.
Now I'd earn mine.

                    I don't complain. It's not
in *Bugle Notes*. And when the shirkers howled
for blood, Styer backed me. I repay
my debts. I do my duty. But a firm
"no" when it's called for opens eyes
and spares us years of chasing "maybes."
I turned the job down flat. So Styer said,
"The president himself approved our choice."
He wanted me put out to pasture. Or
did Stimson, Somervell, and FDR
believe these scientists could boss God's word
and I boss them? Old Pot would say, "That chance
makes even you look slim." My budget topped
six hundred million every month. This job
in all should cost a sixth of that. Or less.
And then, *We've chosen you to field this ball*'s
one way of saying, if this thing goes south
we need a goat. Someone expendable
Congress can sock away in Leavenworth
so deep they'll have to pipe the sunlight in.

That won't be me. Defeat's distasteful. Worse,
it's inefficient. But efficiency
takes guts. Sometimes you have to mortgage souls
to do a job. They've chosen me. I'll see
how terribly they want these "special" bombs.
"You'll need someone to finish up the Pentagon.
I know the senators involved. And their
investment." Styer saw my point at once.
I would, he felt, command the scientists'
respect more easily as brigadier.
They care more for prerogatives of rank
than soldiers. We put duty above all.

Edith Warner

Ran a tearoom by the Rio Grande

Who needed mountains? What use the desert's blank rock silences?
For half my life the city penned my heart—the world beyond it
just geography. Until a sudden illness blighted
my internal neighborhood. My doctor couldn't name it, knew
no medicine but rest. A full year's worth. My parents' friends
had read of German sanatoriums. Mine spun the globe
and urged gay fantasies. Only Charlotte spoke firsthand:
a guest ranch in Frijoles Canyon outside Santa Fe.
"Beans Canyon?" Skepticism was among the luxuries
I'd have to learn to do without in heaven's stony hills.

What devil took me—or what god? Call it New Mexico,
as I did, knowing nothing but the tremors in my heart,
a many-chambered conduit, I learned, for more than blood.

The landscape's nudity surprised me—everywhere bare rock
clothed only in a shift of shadows, sand pooled deep in dry
streambeds, wide gravel washes, deadwood caked with dust, cracked mud,
silt ankle deep in drifts beside the rusted rails. Even
the air seemed naked, stripped of all humidity, crisp, chill,
and intimate. The ranch's battered Packard stuttered north
along a washboard road, turned west, and spun its wheels in clouds
of alkali. The Rio Grande slid like a sleepy snake
so low between its banks the worm-etched wooden trestle bridge
at Buckman siding sang and shrugged its shoulders under us
before I saw a drop of water.
                              Land of absences,
transparent, vast, a bleached skull's hollow eye, a gulf, a gasp,
a window on the void. My flesh drew tight around my bones.
Was this the Canaan I abandoned home for? No. I'd dreamed
a sham. This place was where God rested on the seventh day.

The Packard staggered up a switchback gouged in soft, white tuff
across a mesa's outer face, and as we rose, the world
unfolded like a mariposa lily's golden heart
when clear rain follows years of drought. We reached the mesa's crest
and straddled a deeply rutted track back toward the Jemez range,
through juniper and piñon, stands of arching western pines
that shed sweet-scented needles like a cloak to tamp the dust.
The road stopped at a canyon's edge. A packhorse grazed thick tufts
of grama grass that bowed bright tasseled heads like sieves of light
beside a steep trail down the canyon's wheat and coral walls.
They formed a crescent mirroring a little river lined
with sun-drenched alders and a stone ranch house. That night I slept
in silence I could feel against my skin. I woke to climb
the canyon trail each morning, walk all day among the groves
of scrub oak and majestic ponderosa. Indian
paintbrush and prickly pear, the spiny cholla's fuchsia blooms
led past the cultivated bounds that had defined my life.
The dust itself seemed full of life—not ashes, but dry clay
only wanting rain and artful hands to free its echoes
of eternal forms. I walked home under a descending sun
that brushed fresh fire on the mountains called the Blood of Christ,
as liquid turquoise filled the valley like a rough clay bowl
the way an old man's eyes will brim a last time as he dies.
Our blood is slaked with earth, each vein that feeds our dusty hearts
a trumpet vine entangled in an old salt cedar's arms,
calling the newly faithful to a kind of reckoning.

Robert Serber

Physicist

Oppie and his brother spent their summers
in the Pecos Mountains north of Santa Fe.
They had a ranch they called Perro Caliente—
Katie Page's Spanish double take
on Robert's first words when he saw the place.
In '35 he summoned us to make
the pilgrimage, and though our city blood
felt like the sap of potted plants, I'd learned
to pity men who disappointed Oppie.
So we headed down Route 66,
with Charlotte riding shotgun, primed to find
high mountain meadows, a canopy of stars.
We crossed into New Mexico, and bang!
the highway turned to dirt. We wondered if
we'd underestimated how much zeal
we'd need. We wondered for two hundred miles.
But once we'd passed the cabin and the small
corral half hidden in the aspen, twice,
before we grasped it must be Oppie's "ranch,"
we thought we knew the worst. What did we know?
The place was "picturesque." Two rooms. In one
a battered couch, a Navajo throw rug
beside the huge stone hearth, and that was it.
The kitchen housed a wood stove and a pot
of chili left to ripen all week long.
No sink. No plumbing, period. No place
to sit. They all slept on the bare board floor.
It daunted us at first, until we learned
our worry was unfounded, since a few
"old friends" had happened by that afternoon
(the way Scott must have happened by the Pole)

and commandeered our spots on Oppie's floor.
Instead, our kind host loaned us horses. "Ride
straight north, toward Jicoria Pass," he said.
"Blue and Cumbres know the way." We tried
to smile. "In three days you'll reach Taos, where
they always have a room for friends of mine."
Well, I'd seen photographs of horses, once,
so who was I to look these in the mouth?
We mounted gingerly and said good-bye
to Oppie. Almost as an afterthought,
he handed us a fifth of scotch, a box
of crackers, and two bags of oats. "The oats
are for the horses," he admonished us.
We gave the beasts their heads and off we went
into the Pecos wilderness, two rubes
trusting in God as they had never done before.
By afternoon our fears had eased, replaced
by pain: the stirrups bruised our city feet,
the saddles rubbed our thighs and buttocks raw.
We camped that night beneath the canopy
of stars, but hardly noticed them as sore
legs stiffened, backs cramped, tender blisters swelled.
The first two days remain a nightmare blur.
Then on the third day Charlotte lost her grip
and fell. I ran to help, but she got up,
said she was fine, and seemed to be, except
for what appeared to be a bloody straw
stuck in her cheek. I tried to pluck it out
and found it was a fountain of her blood.
A pine needle had pierced her cheek and hit
an artery. I tore strips from my shirt
and bound her jaw. The bleeding wouldn't stop.
What could we do? We got back on our horses
and urged them on toward Taos. Two hours
later, a cluster of adobe houses

appeared on the horizon. Charlotte broke
into a gallop. When she reached the town
she reined her horse in by a wide-eyed group
of local men and fell off at their feet.
They called a doctor, and he sewed her up.
So ended our adventure: a small taste
of life in Oppie's world, which might, you'd think,
have left me soured on my boss. But no:
we'd reached past every possibility
we had imagined for ourselves, inspired
by Oppie's expectations and his blunt
refusal to allow that we might fail.
He drove us past all inhibition. So
when Oppie called six thousand scientists
together in the Jemez range, among
the cottonwoods above the Rio Grande,
to do his secret weapons work, we came,
trusting what he would make of it, and us.

John Dudley

Major, Army Corps of Engineers

No matter what your weapons are
without mobility you get
nowhere. Gunpowder's grand enough,
but give me the lowly stirrup
and a game horse, I'll have you dine
on dust. Try telling these highbrows.
—They'll hand out x's, y's, and z's
to prove the history books all wrong.
Seems nowhere's where they want to be:
inland two hundred miles or more,
with water for three hundred men,
secluded, ringed with hills to keep
the strangers out, the natives in.
They dream of Shangri-La. They'll wake
to dust nine months a year and mud
the rest. But listen to advice?
At best I'm just a pair of eyes
and half a brain. They calculate
I wouldn't understand their work
or what their precious lab is for.
Odds are it's better not to ask:
they'd never let me leave. And so
I follow every rutting track
from Honey Lake to Hope to Hobbs.
When things get tough, I take a jeep—
or, tougher, stirrups—searching till
I find the perfect spot. Well, near
enough. Jemez Springs in late fall
fits their specs from A to Z—

mild winters, miles from anywhere—
even a ridge to separate
the living quarters from the lab,
in case they take it in their heads
to blow themselves to hell and back.

Edith Warner

Ran a tearoom by the Rio Grande

Luck finds me when I least expect it. Sometimes I have failed
to make it welcome. Poor, the desert of the here and now
lay all around me, bleak, stark, broken only by wild spice
bush, juniper, and prickly pear. I glimpsed the fingerprints
of God and tried to turn away, wanting to roll like a colt
in the lush grama grass of memory's blue rangelands. Bless
bad luck.
                    In Posahcongay, *"where the water makes a noise,"*
the Pueblo men made camp, down from the mountains hauling logs
for railroad ties. They laid the Chili Line from Santa Fe
to Antonito, and where it curves to cross the Rio Grande,
splitting a scraggly stand of cottonwoods, they built themselves
a small frame house—a drab, tan, temporary thing—its floors
and walls of knothole-pocked, unfinished boards rough-patched with tin,
a bleached tar-paper roof, skewed windows, and an unplumbed door.

Some men are moved by beauty; some prefer an easy glut.
The logging done, a Portuguese railman stayed on to guard
the broken boxcar depot run aground beside the tracks
that served as freight drop for the Ranch School at Los Alamos.
He hit up Connell for a watchman's wage and called himself
the station agent, but his living was a bootleg still.
He bought a gas pump and a Coca-Cola sign and sold
drinks, soft and hard, canned food, and cigarettes. He stayed six years,
then disappeared midwinter—just when my poverty
was ripe enough to answer Connell's need.
                                        We like to count
blessings, thank lucky stars; but who can number all the names
of God? The first of May, and spring limped like a patchwork tramp.
I was alone—even my trunks less heavy than my heart.
But work distracts, and heals. I swept, hauled water, scrubbed the floors.

A cold wind whistled through the wallboard gaps. I lit the stove
and set a pot of ivy on the windowsill. My clock
ticked on a box of books. A soft Chimayó blanket turned
a folding iron bed into a couch. Slowly the house
foreswore its dubious allegiances and welcomed me.
In the long hour before twilight, I sat on the steps
and listened to the river. Two great mesas to the south
loomed upward as if drawn out of the earth by ancient spells
the sun had whispered as it swung above their massive heads.
My nearest neighbors lived a mile away across the river.
I thought about the Colt revolver Connell lightly left
propped on a barrel of my mother's plates. "You'll not need this
but might sleep easier if it's to hand." Men place faith strangely.
I'd moved past being saved by men—or any works of theirs.
Madness or desperation brought me here, or so it seemed.
Yet I first heard the river's song that night; and now I dance
the steps for which the gods have shaped my feet. The future sleeps
in secret hollows in our bodies, rising suddenly
as wild geese cross a mesa's rim in long grey lines at dusk.
A flood tide in their hearts sweeps northward.

                                                  Death could be like this.

John Dudley

Major, Army Corps of Engineers

But "Oppie" has his own ideas.
He takes one look at Jemez Springs
and says, "I know a better place."
Like hell he does. And I could spit
when he suggests we drive north
to the ranch school at Los Alamos.
Like no one else has heard of it
or noticed how the sawtooth range
across the Rio Grande turns blood
red in the setting sun. I know
the spot is beautiful, all right—
but beauty doesn't fit the specs
he handed me himself. Plus dicey
water, iffy access roads,
a load of locals to evict,
and all up high enough to give
these longhairs nosebleeds. Now, of course,
he says he wants the site up high
to make it more secure; he says
good roads are optional, so long
as you can haul a howitzer
up there—as if he'd ever seen
a howitzer. But Groves agrees,
and it is pretty clear by now
that Oppenheimer'll have his way.
If I suggest a better place
he'll just rewrite the rules again.

Louis Slotin

Physicist

On the train from Oak Ridge down to Lamy
we talk about our new assignment
at Los Alamos, the doubled frontier
of atom bombs and Wild West escapades.
We savor the thought of living side by side
with pioneers like Bethe, Bloch, and Bohr—
though stuck for hours in the same cramped seats,
our aching backsides make us squirm
and dampen our enthusiasm some.
But still we feign a manly disregard.
So when Bill kvetches at the food, or lack of it,
I mock his daintiness and ask
what he expects when we're at war. I figure
maybe I'll give him food for thought. I say
I was a regimental engineer in Spain
resisting Franco's fascists. This trip is nothing
next to riding in a cattle train turned hell-
hole troop transport from Quinto to Ambite.
The ancient Falstaff-bellied boiler choked us,
coughing coal smoke and a froth of oil.
We had no food at all until we stopped
abruptly by a truck parked in thick scrub
near no road I could see. We climbed out, baked
and aching. Dust had painted us to match
the khaki-colored earth. A troop of cooks
stood by the tracks—a brigade of golems
with grub buckets tilted on their shoulders.
Up and down the train they lugged
the metal pails of rice and beans.
Cup measures dangled from their belts

like sidearms. In our half-starved state,
we saw the flies that swarmed around their heads
glisten like halos in the setting sun.
Funny how time and distance make
privation sound romantic. Bill shuts his trap,
his hunger blunted by a few choice words.

Dorothy McKibben

Manager of Site Y's Santa Fe Office

Each day a stream of new lost souls succeeds
the last. I number the innumerable hosts
in triplicate. My office door should read,

"Through me the road unto a town of ghosts;
through me the way to join an endless war;
through me a path among the Lost Almosts:

Abandon hope, all ye who enter here."
But what it really says is "U.S. Eng-
rs," an unlikely ensign to inspire

the many tribes of man, that motley bunch
of carpenters, machinists, plumbers, cooks,
barbers, statisticians, butchers, spooks, trench

diggers, metallurgists, welders, WACs,
doctors, draftsmen, scientists, and wives
who wash up on my doorstep among stacks

of suitcases and trunks, some only half alive,
some screaming for a missing Van de Graff
or Steinway grand. Most, thinking they've arrived

at last, collapse into a chair and, only half
in jest, refuse to budge. "You're nearly there!"
I point out, brightly, earning a dark laugh.

"Bus leaving for the wilderness up yonder!"
I hustle them outside and pack them in
the army's surplus school bus. The GI driver

ties the front door handle shut and grins.
"The General hisself said I mustn't lose 'em.
Seems they're scarce." I wave and they begin

the long descent, as the desert's dusky hues send
purple shadows up the Pecos and
the Jemez floats in gold. Where Santa Cruz bends

to meet the waters of the Rio Grande
in Nambé Valley, they will turn to climb
the dark escarpment, over coral sand-

stone and old lava beds, white pumice, time-
etched tuff, along a road scrimshandered
in the bones of what one tired soldier termed

"that beat-up land." But my horizon's bounded
by mops and mirrors, boxes, bags, and parcels,
cots, cribs, potted plants, and candles. Stranded

here on Earth, I sort and catalog the mortal
fragments of a flock of scientific gods.
I man the gate, forever at the portal,

paused, poised to ferry, usher, prop, or guide.
I'm operator, concierge, den mother,
babysitter, bus stop, getter of rare goods,

dog walker, comforter, solver of other
people's problems, everyone's best friend.
Fractured by war, which one of us knows whether

we're doing right? I cannot guess what ends
they're aiming for, or if they will succeed,
but I believe they'll make me whole again.

Robert Serber

Physicist; Diffusion Theory Group leader

When Oppie's first recruits arrived in March,
few knew what we were working on. Rumors
stitched bits and pieces of the facts to pure
conjecture: radium-laced poison gas,
electric rockets, windshield-wiper blades
for submarines. So Oppie had me write
some talks to bring our colleagues up to speed.
We used the lab's unfinished library.
While carpenters stomped in and out and cursed
and hammered, hanging drywall, doors, and shelves,
I raised my voice above their senseless noise:

"The object of our work is to produce
a bomb—"
                    But Oppie stopped me cold. He said
I'd better pitch that word. I tried again:

"A gadget of the kind we hope to make
is likely to result in several kinds
of damage, which I'll outline briefly here.
With fifteen kilograms of 25
we can expect that this device will yield
a range of pathological effects
within a thousand-meter radius.
The radioactivity will be
a million curies ten days afterward,
tending to render the locality
unfit for habitation for some time.
The gadget also will initiate
acoustic waves, and their velocity
will superpose on the velocity

with which the vaporized material
will be convected from the blast in jets,
and so the wave will overtake itself
and build a well-defined destructive front.
Thus, if destructive action is regarded
as a function of the pressure amplitude,
it follows that the likely radius
of noteworthy mechanical destruction
will be about a mile. As you can see,
these are not insignificant results.
But they involve considerable cost.
Since the materials this work requires
are precious, they constrain us to maintain
as high efficiency as possible.
Our aim is, simply put, the maximum
release of energy per nucleus."

Who would have thought mere words—so technical
and flat the workmen never blinked—could sketch
the pattern of a star to singe the earth?
Big words will move small men, as Hitler knows.
Cold as dawn, science stirs belief, not faith.

Richard Feynman

Physicist; Diffusion Problems Group leader

Once people thought that angels
beat their wings to push the earth
in its ordained track around the sun
as easily as we might move a blackboard
covered with Serber's latest figures.
That view has now been somewhat modified.

The blank, unassuming face of a blackboard
makes it easier to calculate the sun's
mass, and gravity's figures
speak louder than the handful of earth
in a man. Numbers don't change
their minds, like people or angels.

As a boy, I thought I'd been left on Earth
by aliens. I could figure
the rotational velocity of a changeup,
but my aim was a radian off. While the sun
arced through the blue vault like an angel,
I scrawled resonance equations on a blackboard.

On my first drive up to Los Alamos, the sun
on cottonwoods and sandstone transformed
me. I'd been thinking of Arline
in the TB ward in Albuquerque. The doctors figured
she had a year. My heart was a blackboard
covered in odds. The naked earth

rose before me then like the figure
of an angel.
I could spend my life slaving at a blackboard

and never quantify the way light shifted
in her eyes. I lay down on a bare patch of earth
to think. My chest was heavy with sun.

I chose the smaller job: alter
the course of a war. Armed with a blackboard,
I would earn my place on Earth.
Behind me, an angel
beat her wings. I circled the sun
with a lasso of figures.

Edward Condon

Physicist

Dammit, Oppie's always right. Or right enough.
They cluster at his elbows, tossing back
his ossified martinis, *num num numming,*
as if mere mimicry could body love.
My heart's gone numb. I anchor the couch
and find *The Tempest* open on its arm.
For Oppie, isolation is exotic—
this mesa top, an island in the clouds,
and he, our Prospero. I read out loud,
sweet promises of "riches ready to drop,"
a spell to strengthen faith. He'd have me think
I'm Ariel, a second-in-command
of sorts. Vice-head. Almost associate
director. Right enough. Except that part
is Serber's. I'm more Caliban: so clumsy
that when I sputtered up a vacuum cell
and mirrors in the Berkeley lab, I broke
so damn much glass that Lewis fobbed me off
on Theory.   This bomb is hypothetical.
Who knows for sure what strange things must converge
for it to fly? My work at Westinghouse
on microwave radar was real—a sound,
no-kidding contribution to the war.
And yet most scientists say "industry"
in sharp, stern tones. To them the thing I've done's
unspeakable: tossed in the sponge. I'm like
a fallen woman, bedding capital.
I should have let the universities
make love to me instead. Now watch them trade
their tweeds for khaki. Institutional

love's built on jealousy, and down that street
await the trappings of a fascist state.

"Be not afeard." I mouth the words. But Groves's
bulk blots out sun and casts the page in shadow.
He would redact our very souls, friendships
and loves blacked out by censors' pencil strokes,
our wives kept ignorant as aliens,
all of us thieves in his fiefdom, spied on,
confined to our minds' own cubbies, rendered mute
as black boxes, unknowable except
as cogs that purr or grind in his machine.
As if we weren't already cursed by halves,
like apples split for pickling, or boiled eggs
divided by a hair. Los Alamos
is just a crate we're packed and salted in.

The world is hard enough to grasp without
Groves's "need to know"—or rather, "need not know."
He'd have us waste our days as coroners,
dissecting the corpses of each other's work
the way we cut up Tizard's magnetron
to figure how it oscillates. "It's just
a whistle," Rabi said. But when I ask,
"Then how do whistles work?" he can't explain.
We're each a finite part, and fallible,
in isolation, partial; yet when joined
in science's communal mind, our sum
approaches truth. If we could make ourselves
infinitesimal, we'd know God's will.
Meanwhile, Groves patents even whistles.
                                        So
we bluster, jury-rig, know only half
of what we do. Who can predict such fumblings'
ends? We might as well pretend the world

is just an N-dimensional mess space
with one Cartesian axis for each man's
brute appetite. Borrow heuristic rules
for how much food a ship's cook should prepare,
and the resultant probability

$$P(y)dy = \frac{1}{0.63\sqrt{2\pi}} e^{-1.25(y-1)^2} dy$$

disquiets only in the range that maps
men adding to the mess, disgorging what
they should digest. We're whistling in the dark
like Wilson's "thousand twangling instruments,"
as Oppie calls them. Laughter masks our fear.
Machines these days are so god-awful fast
you just feel like an utter fool.
        And yet
without them I'd be stuck where I was born,
and Alamogordo's hardly any place
to be but "from." Thank God in my first year
my father engineered a rail line out
to Cloudcroft. Right enough. But like a stone
nudged down a slope, momentum is conserved.
The Feather River Canyon, Hoquiam,
Wenatchee, Berkeley till the earthquake kicked.
I can't name half my fourteen grammar schools.
But Dad loved trains; stenography, Mum joked,
wrote her a ticket anywhere. They roamed
the earth until they couldn't even stay
together. Pathologic wanderlust.
Later, I'd kid (my laughter masking loss)
that our nomadic life went on until
my parents had to pay full fare for me.
Until I'm only in my element
when leaving it.
       Physics finds truths mere men
alone could never know. But you must learn
which things to ask. So: Does a birdcage weigh

more when the bird is flying round inside
or on its perch? It's clear we're banished here,
like Prospero, until our art's perfected
and we use it. Does fumbling never end?
I can't stay on. No more of being "old
man" to these snot-faced geniuses. No more
short-handing Serber's lectures like a scribe.
No more denying Emilie a bath
or Mädi school. No gambling my career
on Oppie's being right—gut-sure that dreams'
impossibilities are safer bets.
No more of three hands tied behind my back.
No playing second fiddle till Rome burns.

Louis Slotin

Physicist

I've been called a cowboy by some timid souls
who do their work as though it were a job.
They say I take unnecessary risks.
I say the bantam champion of King's
can be his own best judge of when to duck.
I come from savvy stock. My father proved
our fitness when the Czar's Okhrana forged
their *Protocols*: he bobbed and weaved and fled
the pogroms in Белая Русь and bought
a house on Manitoba's Inkster Street.
I learned from my Отец never to let
a bunch of regulations collar me.
The leash is always held by someone else.

In Oak Ridge, Tennessee, the army built
the largest closed-roof building in the world
to filter handfuls of uranium
235, a rarish isotope,
from its abundant cousin, 38.
Off in a corner of that commonwealth
Wigner ran a prototype reactor
in a fifty-seven hundred gallon tank,
testing techniques to breed plutonium.
One Friday, after weeks of work, we'd reached
the final trial of an assembly
designed to gauge free neutron density,
but counters at the bottom of the tank
required realigning. Morgan planned
to drain and then refill the whole damn thing
for fifteen minutes' tinkering. I said
he must be crazy, but he clung

to the procedures he'd been taught,
though they'd delay the run, and Wigner hoped
to have the weekend to decode the data.
I didn't see the sense in waiting, so
when Morgan went to lunch, I stayed and stripped
down to my BVDs. I will admit
it's tricky working underwater, but
I had those counters humming like a top
when he got back. But did he thank me? No.
He blew his stack and damned me for a fool,
although the radiation never topped
acceptable parameters. Call it
chutzpah or dumb bravado if you like,
I saw a job and did it. Period.
To hell with fear and excess caution if
it interferes with what I know is right.

Peer de Silva

Lt. Colonel, Fourth Army; Head of G-2, Los Alamos

Tigers roam the globe.
Take Hitler's smarter brother, Joe.
His swagger beggars better men's
belief, angers the best.
While Nazis swallow countries whole,
he spews chewed pablum glib
whiz kid atom crackers suckle
like a treacly tit. It devours
their minds until they think
clinking cocktail glasses
mimic worker's hammers
and they wink like bats
at non-aggression pacts.
Their only undivided's
science; they seek no higher
good, believe God speaks
in cyphers only they can read,
as if they're wiser than us
grunts. Naive. Or liars.
Oppenheimer's childlike trust's
the worst. Milk and honey
from some egghead's Eden
where bleeding-hearted
fellow travelers think trust
is "only decent." Blind
faith's poison, even
smacks of treason. Gimcrack,
geegaw sentiment at best:
cheap beads he's set
to trade Manhattan for.
Ideology is war.

His "overwhelming
judgment's" based on hope,
not facts. Only dupes
would let him stack his staff
with apparatchiks—
all the Reds and pinkos
of a communist rainbow—
less covenant than
Russian coven. What's
most vital to these forty-eight
United States? Not
further freedoms
conjured up for comrades
who would feed our secrets
to the Soviets. We need
blunt patriots
with guts and clout
to rule who's in the know,
who on the outs.

Edward Teller

Physicist; Hydrodynamics of Implosion and Super Group leader

Wigwam calls us Martians, jokes
that we Hungarians
are not quite human. Superior,
perhaps. But alien.

My colleagues do not joke. They brand
me outcast: gimp, lame duck.
I'm crippled by their sympathy.
Who hasn't had bad luck?

My Friday the 13th arrived
on Saturday. I hopped
a Munich streetcar; young, I dreamed
of love and missed my stop.

Jumped. Stumbled. Three cars rumbled past.
My boot, spoiled, yards away.
I fretted: could I join my friends
to hike the Tegernsee?

Pain answered. Someone fetched my foot.
Von Lossow cut and stitched,
fused fi bula and tibia.
My calcaneus itched.

Shrapnel-laced soldiers suffer more.
Self-pity I will leave
to those with no ambition and
the time to whine and grieve.

Ruth Marshak

Physicist's wife

Tech was a pit that swallowed up
my husband, day and night, and left
his better half, an untrained soldier, fighting
heartache. Finally I gave up
waiting dinner. Often he came home
at three or four a.m. Or not at all.
He said since all we had were army cots,
he might as well sleep in the lab.
I think the army knew what it was doing
when it only gave us single beds.
What made it worse was that this sacrifice
was not a sacrifice for him. He loved
his work. It overcame all scruples,
all familial feeling. Few of us knew
the thing our husbands sought,
its magnitude, or why it had aroused
such passion. "There's a war on, love," Bob said
each time I asked, until I learned
to shut my mouth, and wait, and spend my energy
on the mechanics of my daily life.
The alternation of the seasons: mud
to dust and back to mud. Teaching
third-grade prima donna kids.
Learning to cook at seven thousand feet
with vegetables and fruits long past
their primes. A total absence
of fresh eggs. I chose my battles. This
was one that I could win. I howled for months
until the army veterinarian agreed
to candle every egg before it hit
the commissary shelves. I'd had enough
of finding grim reminders
of what they wanted to become, and failed.

James Nolan

Captain, US Army Medical Corps; Chief Medical Officer, Los Alamos

What were we making: babies or . . . ? That joke
wore thin, though no one ever finished it.
We read the punch line in each other's eyes,
wanting to laugh but only managing
watered-down, soldierly smiles. Tight lipped, we
walked around towing blank speech bubbles like
wind-fretted barrage balloons. Our besieged hearts
were blacked-out burgs. We hunkered down, silent,
watching G-men in crisp snap-brim straw hats
wooing the thick shadows in every door-
way. So when Weisskopf stormed the hospital
with a letter to his sister some half-
witted censor'd chopped to hell and back and
wondered, really meaning it, "How can you
work in a place like this?," all I did was
wink and whisper, "Mum's the word."

John Dudley

Major, Army Corps of Engineers

By then I'd had it up to here
with stuck-up, smart-ass scientists.
For months I'd asked to join the war
and been mañana'd by the Corps
with lines a moron wouldn't buy:
"Your work here just might win this thing."
And so when Ashbridge turned me down
for transfer—yet again—and said
instead I'd have to babysit
my prima donnas six more months,
I blew my stack. The last three months
had done me in. These scientists
behaved like children—smart as hell,
of course, with all their theories and
the laws of atoms and all that,
but when it came to common sense,
the Lord had clearly passed them by.
Somehow they couldn't grasp the fact
that requisitioning supplies
takes time. They wanted everything
the day before they asked for it.
They didn't even understand
what safes were for. I used to find
thick stacks of classified reports
left lying on their desks, their safes
wide open a few feet away.
And then they'd clam up when I asked
for stats to help me build a shed
to house their darling cyclotron.
Later, I'd find them chattering
like magpies in La Fonda's bar,

discussing secret facts and figures
with a dozen locals listening.
I've had some physics in my day:
it doesn't take an Edison
to figure out that something's up
when words like "fission," "nucleus,"
and "bomb" are thrown around for free.
I tried to tell them even I
was not supposed to know these things.
I couldn't shut them up. Some days
my biggest job was just to keep
their precious secrets from myself.

Bernice Brode

Computer

Mary knows what's what, but she's not spilling
any beans. Just counting them. She lays her
problems in a wire basket: "Free—Take
one!" They mount to heaven, make my Marchant
clank and groan as Oppie struts the hallway,
trailing minions. Always witty, Mici
quips, "There goes the mother hen and all her
chicks." Late-afternoon sun smears like putty
on the windowpanes while Mary fusses
over decimals. "Mrs. B, your errors
are appalling!" I should practice math each
night at home, although my pay stub's only
⅜ time, and asking why the army
favors awkward fractions ruffles feathers.
"Mrs. B, if I knew that, I'd rule this
whole blamed roost." I punch another seven
digits, then another, till a green key
sticks. Gears grind and catch. Unnerved, my figure
jogs the graceful curve our work is tracing.
When he stoops to scan my index card, Moll
Flanders winces, strokes his beard. I wonder
what we're hatching. He won't sing. "This thing we're
doing, if we do it, will begin a
revolution." Then he shuts his beak, *tap-
taps* his pencil—always the conductor.
Tiny pinwheels spin and click. Though numbers
do not lie, they may not be correct. Joe
trained us well. I feel his eyes, vague rumors
whispered through thick lenses, watching still, or
peering at his *Esquire* calendars (tacked
up "for cheerfulness," his Ma might offer,

if she had been cleared to visit Tech). Trust
lays a finger on the scales. To lighten
or to weigh them down? I read the posted
signs—"Keep out," "Wear lead"—and calculate what
all these days we'll live cooped in by fences
add to my boys' lives. My concentration's
shot, my shift is up, and meanwhile Mary's
chirping, "Mrs. B, there is a brilliant
future in computing if you'd only
learn your decimals." I should be patient
but she eggs me on. I let her have it:
"Twenty years ago, I was your age. This
is my future." Dear God, let it count.

Edward Teller

Physicist; Super and General Theory Group leader

Bethe made the Head of Theory?
No matter. Out of all
my Berlin colleagues only he
stopped by the hospital.

Stiff, awkward, mute, he strove to keep
his eyes above my knees.
Now he insists I should compute
implosion symmetries.

I know the endless clanking gears
brute calculations use.
Though others' strengths incline that way,
my genius says, "Refuse."

I offer Oppie this defense:
Productive work's no whore;
a scientist needs faith his math
will influence the war.

Some call me selfish. Moody. Spoiled.
But Oppie bows to reason.
Gives me a group of outcast souls
who know zeal looks like treason.

Klaus Fuchs

Physicist; Soviet spy

> Hitler disliked my politics. He blamed
> the Reichstag burning on my comrades.
> Only Christel and I escaped the flames
> of der Fuhrer's fury. And both of us went mad.

Capital killed democracy. It built
too powerful an engine. Now an engineer
applies the brakes or puts on steam according
to needs of the machine and not its passengers.

> *words are ships*
>
> > *crewed*
>
> *by dead souls*
>
> > *their holed hulls*
>
> *sieves for living*
>
> > *thoughts*
>
> *their only freight*
>
> > *the breath*
>
> *that shifts*
>
> > *slack shrouds*

> I controlled my schizophrenia, but
> Christel had less luck. Cursed by choler,
> she swallowed rubber crumbs from bits
> orderlies wedged between her molars.

Science is of two minds: man and nature
shut in separate hemispheres. One side
lies dormant while its twin sets loose brute forces,
cut off from knowledge of the human cost.

I controlled my schizophrenia, but

In my dreams, Elisabeth still climbs the arc
of the Friedenstrasse bridge, crosses the tracks,
almost, then stops. Cornered by Gestapo sharks,
she jumps. A train rolls by. My vision blacks.

Colonies and taxes, wars and debts,
wherever nations copulate with capital
all their bloated offspring celebrate
Herod's slaughter of the innocents.

to sound such depths
unmans me

My brother asked for agitprop, not cigarettes.
Its jail-yard *Tauschwert* nearly nil,
Gerhard shared it, gratis, with the other "guests."
They couldn't help but live his communist ideals.

Men are not pawns. History owns
no riches, fights no wars. It never in-
vents anything. So how can history
know when to keep or give away a secret?

I bridge
       two headlands
smudged
       by fog
invisible
       to one another
though each
       rocky footing
holds up
       half of me

                    and underneath

                                    the water's

            whispered secrets

                                    set the echoes

            swinging like

                                    a pendulum

            from shore

                                    to shore

                    Father found life too easy as a Lutheran.
                    "Being popular never fostered moral fiber."
                    He scattered aphorisms. "Even a Quaker can
                        value Roman grit." Except along the Tiber.

Though the laws of nature are immutable,
history glimpses their naked forms in different
poses. The wise man knows philosophy
is masturbation, physics rich as sexual love.

            our pasts

                            are patchwork

            fictions

                                    quilted

            out of need

                            and guilt

            When Hans Staub bullied Christel, mother bullied me
            until I fought him. As she knew he would, Hans won.
                Her way was never easy—only once, when she
                    declared, in acid tones, her job was done.

Dead generations weigh like nightmare
on the living brain. The only god, Marx
said, is doubt. It never leaves you, never
cons you into loving it.

what can I do

        but whisper

what I know

        into the gulf

Eugene Wigner

Physicist; Theoretical Group leader, Metallurgical Laboratory

We are all guests
here in this world.
As for the next?
Better, perhaps,
that we not wear
our earthly welcome out.
I learned to love
America in Madison.
Exiled from Budapest
because I wished
to be a physicist,
and from Berlin
by Hitler, then
from Princeton by the men
who coveted my job,
I settled in the midst
of wheat fields in
Wisconsin, fields
like those of Belcza-Puszta
where I learned to talk
when I was three,
laughing at my uncle's
homespun jokes.
In Madison, I learned
another language
from Amelia. She
took me by surprise
not with her beauty but
with love. What curious
animals we humans are
to need romantic love.

But then I've never been
the quickest to intuit
nature's laws. That was
the first of many things
I learned from her.
A few months saw us
married. Then her heart,
which was, I thought,
the stronger, suddenly
went wrong. No one
could tell us why
or how. Nine months
I lived in her
sweet light. I learned
to read by it
my own heart's flickerings.
Then darkness fell,
and I went back to work.

Edith Warner

Ran a tearoom by the Rio Grande

Venus hangs low above the mountains. After a long night's sleep
I feel less like a toy in constant need of being wound.
My headache's gone. My cracked lens bothers eyework, but I read
a little Lattimore. Tilano combs and braids his hair
after his Sunday river bath. The chicken water pans
need cleaning. I will pickle winter pears, tomatoes, squash,
and then lay out tobaccy Dukey, lemons, and sardines
against the herders' ritual return, driving their sheep
down from the pastures of the Valle Grande.

                                          Much I thought safe
is lost already. War drives innovation, justifies
a hasty, thoughtless excess. Dump trucks rut the riverbank:
the army steals its gravel for construction on the Hill
and forces farmers from their bean fields on the high plateau.
Power can be so many things. The rivers, sky, trees, fields,
and even mountains take into themselves what we give off—
and give it out again. Niels Bohr would understand. Last night
his eyes drew fire from the pine knots burning on my hearth—
a golden brilliance that the Israelites thought heaven had—
a light that is the legacy of long-forgotten trees,
the essence of the elements they gathered and release,
a living circle closed. "What lingers in your heart to say?"
I longed to ask, thinking he had a magic word for me.
But now I know there is no magic word—or need for one.
Only endurance, trust. He cannot tell me what they do.

As if he needed to, when Bethes, Fermis, Allisons,
and Tellers dine each night in my tearoom; I recognize
the conversation of atomic specialists; I know
the sound of German and Italian natives, what it means
when such men staff a secret Allied military base.

They think I disapprove. They're right. But not of them.
Last summer Army drillers set up an infernal rig
to test what footing my yard's earth would offer for a bridge.
Fear moved in as a boarder, as it hadn't in past years
when peach trees failed to bloom or hoppers ate the Pueblo crops.
But in the end they oiled the Española road instead.
The gods send fat and lean times. Always rain will follow drought.
But men are slow to learn. They trust their ingenuity;
they think their needs are paramount. And so our Pueblo boys
ship out for England, Africa, and Guam. Hilario
was burned when his destroyer took a shell; Slim saw two friends
draw sniper fire; 5 Cents lost a leg. Pity the soul
who doesn't know enough to disapprove.
                                        This afternoon
we'll spend our rationed gas to gather wood on the plateau,
where sky and aspens vie in beauty. Soon hoarfrost will crisp
the smallest weed stalks, quieting the cries of canyon wrens.
Tonight I'll write a note to Brownie in the Philippines
on Peter's diabolical contraption. What the hunt
system will do to thought's another thing. I promised him.
Tomorrow Kitty comes for vegetables. Pronto will hunt
white turkey feathers with Tilano while our women's talk
brightens my kitchen. Later, Compton, Tuck, and Segre grace
my table. Levity and wisdom, laughter, somber words.
And I will serve them lamb ragout with cloves, posole, sweet
tomato relish in an earthen bowl, and chocolate cake.
My "contribution to the war," they call it. "To the peace,"
I'd say, but don't. I'm grateful for the honor they intend.
I've listened to their talk and learned that what I thought beyond
man's compass can be so strong in some it radiates from them.

J. Robert Oppenheimer

Physicist; Director of the Los Alamos Laboratory

The snows came early & they linger late.
Only the oldest Pueblo men recall
so much, so long. Jean's gone. The sun declines.
Fog gathers in hollows where cool air pools
among the cottonwoods, slowly filling
Water Canyon like a stoppered tub.

Jean disappeared for days. Sometimes for weeks.
Her sleepy eyelid was a veil she longed
to make me long to lift. Concupiscence
& desecration. Laughter. Then she'd wince
& say she'd slept with every bull she met.
Such torment was, to her, love's next of kin.

Since mid-December, Bohr stanched futile talk
& wasted motion, honed our work, our hope
these weapons, wielded wisely, will make war
too horrible to wage. He leaves us soon,
yet waits now while I hike the mesa rim.
A great man recognizes greater grief.

> "Be this my text, my sermon to mine own:
> Therefore that he may raise, the Lord throws down."

Jean emulated slate. The past was chalk.
She chafed, rubbed at her brow to wipe away
the claptrap of her christening. She spurned
my smiling & convulsive frog's-leg love.
But when I left, she wept & wheedled, sent
repentant letters, sparked what I was made of.

> "Trip no further pretty sweeting;
> Journeys end in lovers meeting."

We reunited, solstice fools, in June.
Jean drove her coupe, contralto, top down, crude,
to Xochimilco Bar. She barely flexed
the sacred sphincter of her politics.
We walked in rose & violet fog. I bathed
in her claw-footed tub. She said she'd wait.

> "I mount the stairs and turn the handle of the door
> And feel as if I had mounted on my knees."

Electrons neither move nor rest. The Buddha
gives such answers about death. Camped once
by a cork oak near Corti, I fell in love
by flashlight with mere words. *Le Recherché*:
Indifference to the sufferings we cause
is cruelty, terrible & permanent.

Stenosis stalks us, early, late, a stuck plug
in our guts. But physical, as Bohr once asked,
or mathematical? I couldn't say.
The rock of what the world is made Jean dope
the deep bone ache with Abbot's Nembutal.
I knew no healthy way to be a bastard.

If Jean had crossed the Truchas Peak divide
& sat beneath her horse in pounding rain
& stung her tongue with bitter oranges,
she would have known how lightning scalds the air,
scars earth—how in that fire, her always new
& always moving miseries might drown.

Kitty Oppenheimer

Biologist

Though I was born a German princess and
cousin to Marshal Keitel, my parents left
for Pittsburgh when the First World War began.
Now there's nothing left of my domain, except
a desk they grant me in the lab to keep
me busy studying the fog-bound eyes
and lungs of men who've worked with radium;
or the cocktail parties I'm supposed to give
to boost morale and entertain the guests
some military moron wants impressed.
I ought to laugh at such absurd antics:
like Groves, pretending he's not overawed
by Robert's friends, refusing to undo
his jacket, though its creases make his gut
look like a pregnant sow's. He likes to hand
around their drinks himself, when otherwise
he'd never touch the stuff. He plays the fool.
But so do I: our dear director's wife.
It's grown to be a burden I can't bear.
It used to be just one of Robert's cocktails
made the dullest party come to life. Now
I hardly feel it till I'm stinking drunk.
And when I ask, "How does one get the come
stains off a nightie?" only Robert laughs.

James Nolan

Captain, US Army Medical Corps; Chief Medical Officer, Los Alamos

Petey didn't pity whores. "Son of a . . ."
Pitched low like that, her voice dissolved in growls.
"Peckerhead." She had Groves pegged. His SO
P bypassed morals, even common sense.
Prostitution? If his precious bachelor
physicists pushed hard enough. And how they
pushed! WACs packed my clinic, driven by a
pain "down there," a hellish stench. I calmed them,
plumbed and cultured hurt vaginas, wiped
puffy lips that wept raw umber butter.
Penicillin bought me names. I brought them
post haste to the base CO, whose sworn "I'll
pin those bastards to the wall like bugs" proved
premature. Groves pondered the facts, the girls'
persuasive tears, the young men's equally
passionate appeal, and then our General
pandered to the young folks' "basic needs," though
previously, his stout Victorian
politics taxed Petey's knack for nicknames:
"Pecksniff." "Gigi." "Prissy prima donna."
Pained by the base's birthrate data, he'd
prohibited "all these unauthorized
pregnancies." The wives were livid, or laughed.
Privately, I wished Groves's foolish fiat
possible. The hospital nursery
pilfered beds from other wards; left injured
patients waiting; shunted doctors to new
posts; deferred research; defied the mortal
purpose of a weapons lab. Instead, while
parents dandled puckered newborns, colleagues
proved blast estimates in nearby canyons.

Percussive shockwaves echoing across
Pajarito Plateau shook iron roofs,
preaching the ethics of war, its requisite
productions. Reproduction, sex, love, all
perversions, surplus, excrescences. Yet
piled in bassinets, cribs, bureaus, babies
poured from our assembly line, swaddled in
patinas of grease, bleating like lambs, limbs
plump, sprouting the finest, buttery fleece.

Robert Serber

Physicist; Diffusion Theory Group leader

Most days it was easy to forget
that we were building bombs. In fact, we weren't.
My group in T-Division spent its time
comparing tamper scattering results
from Manley's Cockcroft-Walton measurements
with half-baked estimates we'd jury-rigged
from hunches, gut guesswork, and little more.
Our conversations ranged through new, exciting
territory: spark gap switches, spalling,
mean free paths, backscattering, and neutron
populations. Who had time to talk
of bombs? Technically, the job was sweet
enough, as Oppie said, to put your heart
and soul in—and we did. We took to sleeping
in the lab. Charlotte said she knew the loss
a widow feels. Even brushing your teeth
became a luxury. So when Bob Wilson
put aside his work one winter night
to host a meeting he sententiously
referred to as "The Impact of the Gadget
on Civilization," not many people
took the bait. I wasn't pinched by any
moral qualms, but out of friendship left
a stack of calculations on my desk,
wrapped up in my mackinaw, and went.
Besides, Priscilla told me Oppie planned
to go, and that, as everybody knew,
would make it an occasion.
                                            Incidentals
dominate memory: the cold snap
early in the week that set the sea of mud

churned by autumn rains and army boots
as if in stone, the waning gibbous moon,
and Pegasus high overhead. Inside, the air
was fogged with warm breath as we jawed
in the shadow of the idle cyclotron
about the Nazis' imminent defeat.
Someone alluded to Dumbarton Oaks
and said the new United Nations should
be founded on full knowledge of our work.
But who could tell our story? We were bound
to silence by our army oaths, the slaves
of military secrecy. Then Oppie said,
so softly, so intensely, no one thought
to disagree: "A demonstration. Let
the bomb speak for us." It seemed obvious.
And left us even less time to discuss
the moral ins and outs of weapons work.
We followed Oppie from the lab like moths
drawn by the flame of his sweet eloquence.
Behind us, Wilson slowly powered up
the cyclotron. Its giant magnets hummed
their siren's song. Please God,
we weren't monsters. But we loved our work.

Willy Higinbotham

Electronics Group leader; accordionist

Lightning snaps at the windows. The sky snarls.
Monstrous, magnificent Karloff snarls likewise,
only louder.
A doctor gloats. A little girl will die, will die.
Like us. But sooner. The crowd hunkers, thrilled, thralled,
a blood-hungry crowd.

Fritz carries a torch for his dear doctor,
and waves it.
He'd light the way, jealous of genius
or deformity. These days, no telling them apart.
I try, I try. For the life of me, I—
Science should be an art.

Brittle film stock stutters
on army surplus sprockets   snaps
like Fritz's neck. Another corpse to count.
The masses rumble, restless, threaten thunder,
demand I man my stomach Steinway.
I wheeze. I moan. They stomp and clap.

Spliced, we proceed. Strickfaden's Tesla coils
arc and sputter like first love. Still aglow,
I magicked a bootstrap generator's sawtooth pulse.
Now Oppie sutures me as new group head.
I play along, though in the end I know
a monster burns.

Appolonia Chalee

Maid

Mrs. Fisher's superstitious. She
believes machines clean better than
human hands. She scolds me when
I miss an opportunity
to haul her caterwauling vacuum
room to room, as if my broom
might dirty her linoleum.

Mrs. Fisher still insists her new
electric washer's quicker than
a tub and mangle, though I mopped
all day last Tuesday when it chose
to spew soap suds and dirty water
down the stairs. I tell her discontented
spirits live in these machines, but

Mrs. Fisher twists her husband's arm
to buy more gadgets from the catalogs
Sears sends her. Mr. Fisher is
a scientist. A scientist
I think should know a little better
than to let his wife invite
devils in metal skins into his home.

Edith Warner

Ran a tearoom by the Rio Grande

Over the years I learned their rituals. Tilano joined
the dancers for each new year's festival. On the fourth day
before the dawn the dancers disappeared into the hills.
Slowly women gathered in the plaza. I pressed close
against the wall of an adobe house. They stood in silence,
waiting for the sun to rise above the broad, dark shoulders
of the mountains. The first light seemed to free them, and they formed
a chorus, chanting to the living sun. Its power spilled
into the plaza, filling them. And then the men appeared,
their bodies painted black and white, with mottled turtle shells
tied at their knees and red yarn on their legs, embroidered kirtles
and the skins of foxes, great collars of fir, and feathers bound
into black hair. They moved in unison as animals,
as deer and mountain sheep and buffalo. Their moccasins
beat on the ground with lifted steps that took strength from the earth.
My body seemed to whirl and turn with them, until I thought,
were I an Indian, I'd be a man and dance with men.
But as I watched, I saw their dance revolved around the women,
who softly, slowly, with feet scarcely lifted from the ground,
held men and children, lightly, in the dance. And as they passed,
the women touched the dancing forms and mingled powers
of the earth and sun.
                    But then a distant sound of blasting
echoed from the canyons near Los Alamos. The *tombé* throbbed
and the chorus raised its voice. I watched a long plumed serpent
of grey smoke rise from the hills and spread above the pueblo.

Niels Bohr

Director in absentia, Institute for Theoretical Physics, Copenhagen

Nature is the wildest West.
It promises a world commonly sensed,
but the tale goes south, fast.
Corpuscular and undulatory, light casts
its twinned fields on fields that seem to reflect the tiniest
details, as a screen. Entranced
by clarity, the audience thinks it has witnessed
truth. But like movies, the phenomenal world has convinced
us to prefer faith to knowledge. We may detest
it, but that scoundrels abscond with bound beauties is at least
logical. And a bridge buckling just
as the desperado's buckboard reaches its midst
isn't inconsistent with the mechanics of catalysts.
But when Tom Mix happens past
as Pauline dangles like a well-dressed
pendulum over the abyss, her wrists
gracefully and gratefully acquiescing at the last
possible second to our hero's barrel-chested
yet strangely tender grasp, credence is taxed. Enticed
by narrative, however, we suspend disbelief—for exposed
in this silly fiction is the deepest
fact: particle and wave, dastard and protagonist,
mutually exclusive [   ]s coexist
in every prospect. (A particular word once embraced
favors clarity to truth; scriptwriters must
choose—likewise actors, and us—and so the spiced
tang of absurdity scents the bouquet of our smallest
exploits.) Yet far from albatrosses, these antagonists
are essential to the world's workings. Fullest
(if not full) understanding rests
on acceptance of complementarity. For greatest

of all absurdities is—us: the self-possessed
presence on that space-time precipice's crest,
the observer with insufficient interest
to intervene, yet possessed
of a willingness and—happiest
coincidence!—the means to arrest
these fleeting phenomena and, amidst
the hurly burly, measure and record. Sext-
ants, dumpy levels, calipers, we are obsessed
with instruments that quantify what we've experienced—
in part, of course, because the mind thirsts
to know its habitat, where it might graze or nest
or copulate; but above all things we lust
for the self itself, that innermost
Russian doll. We struggle to touch or taste
a kernel glimpsed
only in the corner of its own eye, encased
in layer after layer of matter, and yet a ghost,
except, like Schrödinger's boxed
cat, in interaction, fenced
in by what it senses, finally deduced
by its own deductive bustle. Squeezed
like a wobbly lush between policemen, the *selbst*'s
reflexive, drunk on circumstance, stimulus-soused.
So much depends on context!
Baker now does what once would have disgusted
Bohr. War makes us ironists.
Sterling souls give way to rust,
and dully mettled men pegged as extras burst
old bounds to shine as stars. Opportunists
or partisans, there's no sure test
to tell an ally from his evil twin. Most
of us are both. Literally. Me. I should have guessed
Uncle Nick would be a welcome guest
among this tribe of outcasts,

where even the pope admits his fallibility. Spliced
from Jewish roots and Christian stock, I taste
in my own mouth's waters mankind's mistrust
of itself, its intermingled but unmixed
springs. Half of me's distressed,
as half of Fermi hopes we fail, aghast
at how eagerly we embraced
our roles as weaponeers. But a physicist's
no more objective or less prejudiced
than anyone—though we, perhaps, resist
a little more the impulse to insist
because to be a scientist
is to be, often, proven wrong. God has diced
with all of us—Einstein foremost, if not first.
Yet, imperfect as we are, fate has thrust
the future of humanity into our hands, coerced
complicity. Knowledge has cursed
us with the power to act, and we have lost
the choice of not to choose. So I have pressed
decent men to dare dark ends, blessed
their descent. They trust
me and find it in themselves to be used
as instruments, knowing the cost
of entanglement. We are this bomb. Its best
ends. And its worst.

John Lansdale Jr.

Lt. Colonel, Field Artillery; Head of Manhattan Project Intelligence and Security

Horns blare. Dust burgeons
in hot air. But the Bakers'
minds are elsewhere.
Crossing Shelby and Water
streets, catty-corner,
against the light, they wander
in imagination's forests,
engrossed in conversation.
Only Agent Maiers's
clever intercession, snarling
traffic with his Packard,
saves them. They saunter
on. Expert in certain
fields, like all their sort
they badly blunder
in believing they are
competent in others.
Lacking worldly
wisdom, they favor
naive and dangerous
routes. We can't humor
such conceits. Hitler's far
ahead of us. Better
to assume the worst
and keep them under
wraps, corralled
behind barbed wire,
phones tapped, mail censored.
One does all sorts
of nasty things that war
requires: the welfare

of a state's worth more
than a thousand longhairs'
mere comfort.
Still: we need their tender
brains in working order.
The Bohrs are harmless—
even charming
in their way. If they adore
their little walks, this officer's
prepared to pamper
their peculiarities,
even to spend considerable
time behind them, careful
to keep them careless,
free to imagine they're in charge,
but always, on my watch, secure
as babes in arms.

Kitty Oppenheimer

Biologist

Now morning sickness is the proof of love—
I'm sick to half past death of proving it.
I should have swiped his badge, not let him in,
but I'd go mad not knowing if he sees
the beauty he once said he saw in me.
Or am I what they say: an aging bitch
who's gotten knocked up one too many times?
At least he saves his better entrances
for me, arriving late at parties, arms
too full of flowers. Their scents intensify
the pale-blue iris of his eyes. He thrusts
them in my arms, as if it were a loss
our laughter at this joke repaired to say
he knows I was deflowered years ago.

All day, I dress myself in memories;
they cut my circulation like a girdle,
and when I talk, a numbness haunts my lips.

Dorothy McKibben

Manager of Site Y's Santa Fe Office

We mustn't speak of doctors. "Physicist"'s
become a taboo word. Family, neighbors,
friends can't know the great men in our midst.

So Nobel laureates, once through my door,
are slapped with noms de guerre. I joke they've been
demoted. "No, Professor, down here you're

just 'Mister.'" You learn quickly who's thin skinned
when Fermi's "Farmer," Oppie's "Oberhelm,"
and even a giant like Niels Bohr is pinned

as "Uncle Nick." But when the devil whelms
my better sense, I can't help feeling crafty:
I glance around, then grab a fitting victim's

sleeve, begin to speak, but stop, look left
and right, then raise one brow and whisper tensely,
blowing through my teeth, "Are you a phhhht?"

Some human things can't be enclosed by fences,
however hard the army tries. Humor
for one. Or memory. There's no defense

against our own minds—false fears' evil rumors
refuse to be rooted out, much less the true.
I've seen how doubt spreads, fast as Joe's tumors,

how fried eggs mounded on my plate grew
cold the morning Nazis marched on Holland.
Camped above the falls at Havasu,

Cady, Eliot, Aline, and I sat stunned.
The radio chirped on. The sky was blue
and just as bright. Frogs' backs still glistened

in the brook's clear waters, and wild celery strewn
along the banks waved jade stalks, as before.
The world appeared unchanged. And yet I knew

nothing remained as it had been. No more
was I to dream of everlasting peace
beneath a piñon tree. A far-off war

had somehow marred the desert's raw-boned grace—
though for a time, the cancer wasn't plain.
Then bulldozers arrived and haven't ceased.

The questions history poses sometimes shame
even an army's strength, yet she insists
we answer, in the end, in our own names.

Antonio Martinez

Laboratory Assistant

Crisp, starched   khaki boxes
my shoulders arch.   Anglo women
stare. "He's beautiful!"   Anita glares.
I wink and laugh   to reassure her.
"It's just the uniform."   More honestly:
she pays a price   for my army pay.
Such honesty's   unwelcome now.
Her jealousy is just   a gesture: it signals
love. Her worry   isn't really real.
She thinks I'm used   to playing manikin
equally in boots   or moccasins.
And yes, I dress   the soldier's part,
defend the white   man's world as if
it were my own,   allow my wife
to dream white   women envy her.
But when I wear   headdress and face
paint for a festival,   when tourists crowd
the pueblo crowing   in delight, in which
world do my eagle   feathers pinion me?
Anita readily   admits Los Alamos
is ugly, but   she likes our hutment's
ice box and extols   the fresh linoleum.
In San Ildefonso,   Mother favors
her mud oven's   vagaries above
the evenness   of an electric stove.
She will not buy   her clay. She stacks
old license plates   and army mess trays
around an iron grill   to make a kiln.
Under her hands   time sits still.
Up on the Hill   Hans Bethe hopes
to stretch the RaLa   sitting time

to milliseconds.   I hammer sheets
of copper for   the pit mockup.
Oppie stops in.   His eyes pace
like a skittish   filly before
he gallops off   to check Omega.
Some days I feel   that restlessness.
Then, when Anita   and Hans can spare me,
I ride along   the Rio Grande
to Santa Clara   where I gather
fresh volcanic ash   for flux that Mother
calls "blue sand."   Back home, we sit
outside her door   and mix clay slips
or cut *kajepes*   if the gourds are dry.
When I ask her why   she signs her name
"Marie," she says,   "That's how the Anglos
know me: now   'Maria' sounds
like someone else."   "Poveka" is lovelier,
though habit turns   all things to English,
and "Pond Lily"'s   not her, either.
She understands   we serve a larger
thing: something   that makes us
strong—or, if we   fight it, breaks us.
It might be called   community.
But which is mine: the pueblo or
Los Alamos? The mother   I've been given
or the wife I chose?   How can I bear
a Spanish name   and speak in English
yet keep my Tewa   soul? I need
the patient, clever   red fox, luck.
I hammer copper,   grind new bearings
for the Van de Graaff.   In October
I return to dance   the harvest festival,
help Mother dig   and sieve her clay.
She offers cornmeal   for the earth's blessing;
we fill a dozen   flour sacks to last

the year. Her pots   are always waiting,
some signed Marie   and others Poh've'ka,
Marie / Popovi,   or Maria Poveka.
I stack the logs,   pour kerosene,
and layer dung   along the edges.
After they bake,   I smother the pile
with ash and fine,   dry horse manure
and let it smoke   an hour. As Mother
pulls the kiln   apart, I look
to see which names   survived the fire.

Kitty Oppenheimer

Biologist

"Hell yes, I have ID." What did he think:
I'd carry it around on top of this?
As if my belly wasn't proof enough
of who I am. And yet the damn kid seemed
convinced that I was carrying a bomb!
These days I can't get in my own front door
without the say-so of some army fool.
But what was he afraid I'd find inside:
what kind of rubbers our director buys,
or why the damned things didn't work?
I would have fainted if I'd had the time
to play at being helpless: but the dust and heat
were killing me. I'd take a hangover
before this, any day. At least the pleasure
wouldn't seem so far away. But when I said,
"I need a drink," I must have looked the part:
he wrote me out a temporary pass
as proof enough for him, if no one else.

Chien-Shiung Wu

Physicist

"Damn kraut." Dumb kid missed
Wigner's accent, birth, beliefs,
everything but him.

Our bodies dog us,
damn us, graph a history,
a map fools misread.

Memos choke my room.
Stacked calculations mock me
with mute paper tongues.

I hide in the lab.
The cyclotron's magnets sob.
Sober men hear it.

Under unstained steel
skin—crisp, featureless—a warm
uranium heart.

Crowding the gauges
to see B Pile's infant pulse,
we preen, proud parents.

Isotopes appear
as twins to other atoms.
We separate them.

Scant hours scotch success,
shame sham pride. The pile shuts down.
Stubborn. Mute. Stillborn.

Fermi: "Ask Miss Wu."
A pause. Awkward swallowing.
To know what I knew.

A harmless mother's
daughter fission products could
devour neutrons.

I^{135}
decays. Newly made, Xenon
eats two long years' work.

My heart's branched veins ape
an isotope chart. They'll strip
me bare to fuel bombs.

Fathers and sons leave,
corpses come back. Three colleagues
kill me with their eyes.

Spit-slurred words ripen.
What wise men would not utter,
my heart's beat repeats.

Fermi says, "The team
needs you." Is this fame, or shame?
Parity's a myth.

Choose both, or neither:
the cloud chamber's fog, the spark
of an electron.

In the lab, facts speak
for themselves. I'm a fool who
repeats what she hears.

Like a dear old friend
β-decay betrays me,
answers honestly.

Donald Mastick

Chemist

Wonder of the work:
to hold rarest earth—atoms
fewer than angels on a pin's head
dancing. Wahl caught
the first chance trace;
now they grace, in all
the world, this vial.
Wahl watches my bushy tail.
Cradling the glass cheek
warm as a cow's teat,
I decant acid must.
Air scrubbers hum, number
every mote of dust.

Crisp snap and the vial neck
cracks. Vapor's invisible
fingers strong as pry-bar steel
wedged in theory's vacuum
heave. Glass shatters. Blunt
splatter laves lips, graves
shadows on my open
mouth's cave walls.
Reflex lick of sour
spit from split lips
swallows the sum
of three months' work,
all mankind's plutonium.

The courtyard's thick
with August dust haste
raises but barely tastes.

Hempelmann's aid is first
and last. I cast my upper lip
in bronze. His quivers
like wax in summer sun,
commands a trunk line,
stat. Oak Ridge mumbles
in the distance, chokes
on static. His voice grows
close and quiet. I've downed
ten times a lethal dose.

My body's sawed from raw
pine boards. Heartknock
heavy as jackboots
shudders my chest's hollow
casket. A weaker man
would weep. I swallow
a throat-plug lump and smile.
Swallow his sodium citrate rinse,
bicarbonate, a rubber tube. See
what a stomach pump can do?
And do. And do. A weaker
man would weep, handed his guts
in a four-liter beaker.

Waffles proffered as a salve,
then Dr. Sippy's powder cure.
I divvy 49
from what was once pure
me—"There's no one else with
your experience"—a distinction
I might wish to live without.
Retorts bubble. Misgivings.
I focus on the chemistry
of resonance, reduction—

until the Geiger-Müller brays:
my breath so hot it pegs
the gauge six feet away.

In theory I'm already
dead. Lucky
life's empirical. And still,
and still, my blood's lit up.
I spit and piss raw
metal. Safer to be
a lowly stock clerk yet
than in the lab's front lines.
Better to bet my ashes' worth
on Wendover, even
live without wonder,
than body miracles
six feet under.

Richard Feynman

Physicist; Diffusion Problems Group leader

Man's main concern is man—so artists
in the Renaissance believed. Scientists
think otherwise. Like bloodhounds
we sniff out invisible codes:
what goes on under the hard
surface of nature. *Mycobacterium tuberculosis,*

for instance. That bacillus broke the code
of Arline's body so badly she spit blood
on the collar of her nightgown. She tried hard
to hide the stains. She fooled the doctors.
For months they thought she had Hodgkin's.
They like to say that diagnosis is an art.

Once I read a book on bloodhounds
while the doctors fussed over Arline's tubercles.
It made those mutts seem like artists
with their noses, but I wondered how hard
it could be. I spent weeks sniffing out their codes,
crawling around on all fours, like a scientist.

Sometimes, I admit, I try too hard
to pass the time. Arline is the real artist.
Each week she mails me a new code.
She won't let me pity her TB
by pretending to be stumped. "You're not a scientist
if you can't be dispassionate." I'm a good dog;

I let her lose. We watch the TB's
progress. It has become a kind of code
of honor for me as a sissy scientist

to match her artistry
in dying, to not let on how it dogs
my dreams. She hates when I take it hard.

So I devote myself to the science
at hand. I ride my assistants so hard
they call me TB
(That Bastard) Feynman. But mostly I hound
myself, as if perfecting the art
of killing might help me crack death's code.

Louis Slotin

Physicist

My work requires grace. It daunts some, sure.
Feynman himself dubbed my experiments
"Tickling the Dragon's Tail." The theorists know
in theory how these active elements
behave—or misbehave—as they explode.
But someone has to test their bright ideas:
how quickly slower neutrons multiply,
which tampers we should use, even the mass
a bomb requires—it all involves guesswork.
At first when every microgram of twenty-
five had fifty people clamoring
for precedence, I used uranium
polystyrene pseudospheres. Then Cy Smith's men
hot-pressed two nickel-plated hemispheres
of Hanford's delta-phase plutonium
set in a half shell of beryllium.
The trick is lowering an upper shell
until it nearly rests against its mate.
With too much space, no chain reaction—but
too little and I'd rather hold a bomb.
"Some delicate adjustments are involved,"
as Oppie says. No wonder I decline
the gross mechanical contrivances
my colleagues recommend—their winches, clamps,
and thumb screws—favoring my hands: I hold
the shells together like a Frankenstein's
oyster cupping a plump, plutonium pearl,
then slowly let the metal mollusk close.
The Geiger counter stutters, clears its throat,
and starts to chatter. So I keep it calm
by holding a slot-headed driver wedged

between the shells, a single metal blade
dividing life and death. One slip could send
the whole assembly supercritical—
a sudden spray of neutrons in the gut
and then the long, slow, agonizing wait
as one by one my organs turn to mush.
Yet in these moments, I feel life and death
so fully, so intensely, I am past
all fear. I hold a rough beast in my hands
and hear its infant prattle, half amazed
how mild it is and, till it recognizes
its own essential terror, beautiful.

Kitty Oppenheimer

Biologist

When Robert planted Peter in my gut
at first I felt a flag unfurling. "Claimed,"
my heart said. "Yes," my mouth. A month alone
in Reno earned our marriage, my divorce.
But when fulfillment? What euphoria?
I waddled like a penguin, body gone
all belly, certain I could never love
the slow explosion of these clotted cells,
convinced I would have more luck mustering
maternal feelings for a stone I'd swallowed.
But earth's own mineral accretions smacked,
at least, of duty I could stomach—some.
Then Pronto stalled: still as a granite chunk
he granted my desire, stubborn, sunk
deep as a fault line in my body's crust.
The doctors heard my pleading in the end,
cleft muscle, parted layered fat, and dug
down, lifting free at last the little boy
who waited, smeared and dripping, at my core.
And when I woke, drugged, sluggish, savoring
the sudden emptiness, I swore no man,
no god, not even Robert would seduce
the She in me again.
                    Now this. Tyke proves
I am the slave of what is possible.
No one can silence nature. She inscribes
her secrets in our flesh: new tissue blooms
with meanings we can't read, but sense. Genes spell
dependence that our lives sound out—small signs
of larger purposes—prolific and
devouring.

What we make consumes us. Tyke,
conceived in disbelief, resists confinement,
scratches the greasy membranes binding us,
fights, furious and futile, kicks and twists,
ties knots in my intestines, spends her waste
into my veins. I long to help her, calm
choked motions, still her strangled gestures,
but both of us are trapped like rats inside
the blood-filled bag my body has become.
Each night, I listen to our heartbeats fight
like bitter lovers, waiting for her rage
to build until she finds the strength to tear
her way out, split me open, spill us both
into a harsh and unfamiliar light.

ΔH

Rose Bethe

Head of Los Alamos Housing Office

We beat the Nazis on a Tuesday
and the lab boys threw a party that same night
as only they knew how.
The theorists were good company, of course,
but lived too much inside their heads
to organize a party on the scale the day deserved.
And yet I didn't want a drink that night.
Not that I wasn't glad
the Nazis had been crushed—their souls
belong in hell—
and not that I was sad
to see my birthplace brought to ruin,
though I was.
My mood was hardly personal.
I felt—how can I say it?—
not beside myself exactly,
but beyond the luxury
of antique notions of the self.
The Nazis forced us here, Gentiles and Jews,
Americans and Russians, Germans, Dutch.
They made us all commit our lives
to evil. Which, with a will, we did.
Grant this once there is a God,
so God may grant we chose the lesser sin.
After the party, we went back to work.

Joseph Rotblat

Physicist

Spay nature. Speed
the spray of neutrons—
prompt, delayed.
Halt fission. Feed
it salt of boron—
scattered, stalled.

       Vain wish. Chiggers,
       sharks reign. Men. Life sows
       selves, greed, pain.
       Looms lust. Prefers
       ripe wombs to calm—blows,
       grapple, bloom.

Silence science.
Defy fact. Ignore
ears, hands, eyes.
Scrap evidence.
Unmap Einstein, Bohr.
Knowledge traps.

       Worse: when Brits thought
       Hitler's tanks were fake,
       missed panzers.
       Furor, flaws, faults,
       seizures, gaffes—mistakes
       science cures.

Leave the lab. Seek
naive work and save
the heart. Grieve.

Bless lost years. Speak
low, less. Count light waves'
darker crests.

> Humble doctors
> succumbed. Proud, they placed
> faith in sums.
> Fascists. Better
> self-shush than bomb blast,
> hush of ash.

John Dudley

Lt. Colonel, Army Corps of Engineers

In Luzon, everybody thought
they knew what we were waiting for.
Each day fresh rumors made the rounds.
We walked the beach imagining
Japan. The first wave was to last
three weeks. Three hundred thousand men
would die. Ten million Japs. I built
a warehouse for the body bags.

George Kistiakowsky

Chemist; Explosives Division leader

I don't know much about luck,
the theorists say—conveying
several tons of high explosive
down the rutted switchback track
from Shangri-La toward Trinity
at midnight, Friday the thirteenth.
But when I taught them poker
and we counted up the chips
they groused until I quipped
they'd cough up more for lessons
on the violin. Great minds
learn fast: my nights' accounts
grow slim. Luck's like
a drop-dead dame—not good,
not bad, though in an instant's
intercourse she'll let you dream.
And then she'll flip you head to heel.
That much anyone can see.
But if we understood the whole
shebang: no need for Trinity.
There's always more to physics
than the eye can know. How tires
hug a curve and bodies sway,
we calculate from friction's tithe
of gravity, till some fools swear
skill's the gal they're going to wed,
the only faithful she there is.
But still we ride on air.
Thank God or bless the army
that maintains the truck, we can't
court luck. And yet we do not dare

ignore her or reduce her
real resistance to a coy
machination of chance.
There's reason for my choice of times—
as bastard physicists should know—
the unavoidable parameters
of production and demand;
almost no decision, no unknowns
to balance but the ones my choice creates;
almost for that reason choosing
midnight, making luck's decision
mine. On this Jornada, death's
the only wager smart men make,
as even physicists will witness,
crossing a desert, in the dark,
where every atom's splitting
and each spark that jumps the gap,
the rain that falls or fails, all laws
of physics will be just our luck—
and then our history.

Louis Slotin

Physicist

The core assembly was as riveting
as watching someone bake a birthday cake—
at first. I did the whole thing sitting down.
And yet the smallest details somehow still
seem luminous. The table top was masked
with long, brown sheets of butcher's paper strewn
with the gadget's gold- and nickel-plated guts.
It felt as though I moved in thickened light,
each gesture so precise it almost hurt,
shifting the metal parts as others watched.
My focus narrowed to a walnut of
beryllium. I cupped it like a yolk
between two hemispheres of hollowed-out
plutonium, womb-shaped, as warm as flesh
from random fissions. Then the tamper's curved
plum-colored calyx closed to form a bud.
I felt a world take shape between my hands.
The Geiger counter clicked. My palms grew slick.
My fingers tingled, slowly growing numb,
gripping the heavy chunks, more dense than gold.
I shifted my grip abruptly. Everybody
jumped. My back ached. Were my fingers freezing
or on fire? I tried to blink away the sparks
from my exhausted retinas. I leaned
close to the sphere, only to see it shrink
to a speck far out of reach. Or had it swelled
to planet size? Great jagged mountains stabbed
my hands—yet smaller than a single pin
between my fingertips. And I began
to fall. I closed my eyes. My stomach lurched.
The taste of rotten lemons stained my tongue.

The core gone critical. Air glowing blue
as radiation ionized my eyes.
Now I would die.

                    Then Serber spoke. "Louis,
are you all right?" He touched my arm. My eyes
were wet. I opened them. In my clenched hands
was the completed core. It seemed that I
was not among the ones about to die.

Dorothy McKibben

Manager of Site Y's Santa Fe Office

How near we are to dying every day
is kept from us—but barely, badly. Joe
died long and hard, and still I couldn't say,

"My love, it's hopeless," even though I know
he knew: night sweats and fever, back pain—all bad
liars. Lots worse than me. I smiled some, showed

my brave face, wished sometimes the TB'd had
the grace to finish me. But life's a job
at which we amateurs must earn our bread.

Few have the guts to quit. The rest cobble
together. . . . It's like boys at play. Brilliant,
perhaps, but no less boys. Even Robert—

something clumsy and endearing haunts
his most graceful gestures. Something dangerous.
But only to himself—because what daunts

strong men, he does. I've watched a stranger trust
him at first glance. I've been that stranger, seen
him walk so that he hardly scuffed the dust.

The element of earth is feeble in
him. Lean at best, he's grown rail thin, frailer—
almost ghostly—than he's ever been.

It's overwork—along with Kitty's failure
to keep him fed. And now the chicken pox
has laid him low—a child's disease. Paler

than a medieval saint bound in the stocks,
he lies in bed, unshaven, gaunt, and weak.
His voice too faint to follow far, he talks

and talks, while scarlet pustules crust his cheeks
and weep. His moon-bright eyes look through me now,
as if I had gone ghostly, too. He speaks

again, beckons me closer. "We will know . . ."
I miss the last word. "Soon"? Or "sin"? Alas,
my boy! You sacrifice yourself to know

secrets God hid deep in the heart of mass—
secrets we may depend on but should never
bring to light. Nature's skin's not made of glass.

Yet what choice has war left you but to sever
the veil, for once and all? You will because
we need you to. Your luck is to be clever

enough to save the world. Also your curse.
Sometimes, despite how fervently we pray,
the only way to save ourselves is loss.

Norris Bradbury

Lt. Commander, US Navy; Physicist

Some things you can control
          and some you can't. But luck
is physics, nothing more.
          Except a million hours
sweating details, second-
          guessing snags and foul-ups,
anticipating every
          accident and glitch.
Too late to worry once
          the hot run starts, so rig
the game up front: Scotch seal
          the booster holes and box
spare castings to replace
          the dummy trap door plug,
then jacket the gadget tight
          in Butvar water-proof.
Once settled in its cradle,
          a simple canvas tent
will ward off dust and rain
          as tamper people jib-
hoist polar cap and plug,
          insert the active core.
At 1600 hours,
          G-engineers chain tongs
to tent peak, latch the trunnion,
          lift and turn the sphere
to fit the shaped explosives
          (as slowly as they wish!).
A shim stock shoe horn's handy
          and a hypodermic grease gun.
Up on the tower top

                the detonator group
will safe the unit's cables,
                switches, and informers.
Where they get the springs
                and fittings is their business.
Jercinovic will bring
                a small dishpan and footstool.
Once the gadget's live,
                we'll spend all Sunday rubbing
rabbit's feet and finding
                four-leaved clovers. Perhaps
I'll bring the Chaplain down.
                And then, come Monday: Bang!

Edward Teller

Physicist; Super and General Theory Group leader

Our drab green school bus shudders, shimmies
like an angry rattlesnake
racing south, toward a desert laced
with dangers and mistakes.

I nudge a dozing Serber, risk
his wrath to ask (he knows
the desert) how to treat snake bite.
He snaps, "A fifth of whiskey."

It's late. I ought to let him sleep.
But I persist, "And if
our bomb ignites the atmosphere?"
He turns his back. "Two fifths."

Frank Oppenheimer

Physicist

LeMay's been roasting towns again.
He isn't vengeful. "No point
slaughtering civilians
for the sake of slaughter."
But he's pragmatic, thinks
civility's a thin veneer
when women and their kids
run cottage industries
in weapons, ammo, even
planes. "We know we'll kill
a lot of kids. Got to be done."
A sea of ruin, a little forest
of drill presses poking
through the thin veneer
of bodies and burnt homes.

———

In lulls between cloudbursts,
we set off smoke bombs on the cliffs.
They lift thick corkscrew tails,
tracing the wind's shifting trail.
Which routes across the desert
will escape fallout? All night
rain drums and puddles on
parched earth. The spadefoot toads
rejoice. Bell voiced, they serenade,
mating in the sudden mud.

———

Robert couldn't be humdrum.
His sunsets always were the best.
Whole summers he had us live
on peanut butter, jugs of bootleg
whiskey, sacks of sausages.
On pack trips in the Valle
Grande, the deer flies stung
like bees. We set the horses on
a full wild run the whole caldera's
two-mile length. We overtook
each other, turn by turn,
to pass the flask like a baton,
downing welcome swigs.

———

Excelsior and raw
deal boxes wait below.
Nailed with corrugated
iron strips, they simulate
the fragile houses we
will soon obliterate.
How badly or how well
my mock-ups should reveal.
I wait and pray LeMay
will soon be obsolete.

———

Groves calls my tests
tomfoolery. That's more
or less what science is
—at best, at least—
since Robert fled to Harvard
leaving both his microscope

and me. One looks around.
Somehow I'd never heard
of sperm. A marvelous
discovery to see what
multitudes one's body births!
Although eventually one wonders
how can nature countenance
such countless deaths?

Donald Hornig

Physicist

The cradle rocks
ten stories up: a corrugated metal shed
bolted to a surplus Forest Service tower.
Lopsided, swaddled in wire,
a bomb's blunt muzzle snuffles
the electric air.
                Martyr,
Kisty called me when the mock-up
failed and Oppie flared.
A dummy weapon with a real
spare spark gap switch
I never should have volunteered.
But it was gorgeous work,
and I was proud: the long shanks
of its axial electrodes
sealed in glass—a flower
only meant to open
once. Then everyone
thronged round with cameras,
timing circuits, tampering
and testing till it failed.
All faulted me.

That cloud hung overhead for days.
No sleep. Not even after Oppie
called his hot shots in: the muckety
muckiest group I've ever seen.
They wouldn't let me touch
the botched X unit—cracked
it open like a corpse
and found it had been fired

three hundred times and more
before it funked. No fault of mine,
they might have said.

The wet wind wails and sucks
air from my lungs.
The steel-lipped doorway
mouths a black sky stitched
with white-hot tungsten sutures.
My heart ticks faintly
counting down.

There's me—and then there's Oppie.
I say: when a thundercloud sweeps overhead
the shadow of one hundred million volts
will crawl across the desert after it;
let's build a ladder for the lightning
with a bomb on top. Madness.
So I thought he ought to think. Instead
he nods, says it's a go. Of course
it goes. And I go up one hundred
rain-slick rungs, his Isaac,
sacrifice to sleep-starved fantasies
of sabotage. The desert's underwater,
roads are muck, trucks
mired in gullies, swamped and ditched.
Our patchwork Armageddon's safe—
from tampering, at least.
The real threats, I can't stall:
where our own error strikes
or massed electrons fall.

Lightning smacks the ground,
scars earth, pocks rock, cauterizes
like a fallen star. I count the miles

by fifths, too few, until I hear
untold, untellable atoms
bully back into the vacuum
panic left. Seared sagebrush
spices air. Creosote and cinders.
Beside me, our beast slumbers
fitfully, its heart
a metal fist. Half mine,
its brain revolves in vacuum,
a glass capsule cupping nothing
but expectation of a swift
electric surge.
                I play the odds
of pleasing Oppie off against
my death. Or do I give devotion
to this bud of my ambition
that blooms in thunder soon?
Either way, I call it love.

Edward Teller

Physicist; Super and General Theory Group leader

It's midnight. Raining. But I smear
sun ointment on my skin.
Dark glasses, welder's goggles, gloves,
a hat. The others grin.

Our bodies are imperfect, yes.
Expendable, maybe.
In time. I know this more than most.
So does our enemy.

The broadcast stalls at minus 5.
The rest lie down. Their feet
point toward the tower twenty miles
away. I choose to sit.

Face forward. Stare down doubt. Fear. Night
trebled by darkened glass.
Soon light will prove my theories right.
I'll make day break at last.

Leslie Groves

Major General, Army Corps of Engineers; Military Head of the Manhattan Project

Stick to your knitting. Nobel physicists
should know that. Not my lot. Even Fermi
began a betting pool, offering odds
our gadget will ignite the atmosphere,
wipe out the world—or just incinerate
New Mexico. A joke, to smooth frayed nerves,
says Oppenheimer. Calculated humor's
smart—in smallish doses; helps your men
defy their fears. But this? Frivolity's
the danger here, not death. Safe in their lab,
they hazard nothing. Headaches. Writer's cramp.
And yet the scuttlebutt these longhairs flog—
that my incompetence once killed a man.
I'd like to see these know-it-alls make hay
with World War I stock blasting caps, fuse cord,
and TNT.
        Midwinter in Vermont:
Winooski's foot-thick ice floes throttling
the pontoon bridge my commandant had built
all wrong. My orders: clear the ice. All wrong.
We cut three-minute fuses, hard to light
or know if they were lit. The cold. The wind.
And Littlefield beside me when the block
exploded in his hand. Tore off his arm.
I knew at once he wouldn't live. I woke
next morning in the hospital, too doped
to mourn, his bone shards lodged like shrapnel
in my left forefinger knuckle.
                Gossip. Spite.
These coddled scholars strut their ignorance.

The bungling's theirs. My competence is all
that keeps their precious keisters in one piece.
I cleared them Triple A priority
when Ike and Mac both thank their stars for less.
If they knew what explosives really do
they'd shut their traps for good and tight.

Last night

I called the governor—another duck lined up.
Shocked silence crackled back along the wire
when I said, "Martial law may be required."
Then anger when I wouldn't tell him why.

And now the weathermen are dithering
amid the hubbub at base camp. Hubbard
and Holzman, rattled by their failed forecasts,
flip-flop and bicker. Distant thunder bombs
the mountains. Experts second-guess themselves
to death. No guts. No choice but to dismiss
the both of them and make my own predictions.
I've trusted general knowledge all my life.
"The devil catch an idle man, he'll find
him work." My parents kept me busy, warned
against the vice of foreigners, the sloth
of other races. They were right. The whores
in St. Supplice thronged every corner, clutched
my sleeve and fawned. No wonder France succumbed,
attacked by Huns. Venereal and pompous.
Even the Mona Lisa proved as ugly
as I thought she would. I wouldn't bet on God's
forbearance. We have marred his work past bearing.

But Armageddon is our least concern.
This bomb's more likely to go belly up.
And what would Fermi care? It's all some great
experiment to him. If Trinity's

a bust, it will have proved the world is safe
from atom bombs. He's not the one they'll hold
accountable for all those wasted billions.
All those years. Me, I'll grow old and lean
as Rayburn, Barkley, Bridges pick my bones
in claustrophobic subcommittee rooms.

Six Schraffts if it's a dud. Indulgent, but
my right hand knows what's what: to Mrs. O
my gut's a favorite tease, yet for this trip
she tucked an extra box of crunchies, creams,
and cordials in my kit, and didn't smirk.
The extra pounds won't nudge scales weighted down
by history. By failure. Fat will be
least of my burdens.
                       Facedown on a tarp
gone slick with drizzle's neither comfortable
nor dignified. But if it's good enough
for Harvard's president. . . . Our feet aim straight
at Zero, like twin compasses. Ten miles.
And if that's not enough, whoever's left
will raise a statue, one day, in our names.

It only takes one soaked electric tie,
one short, and half the world's plutonium
is scattered to the wind—and still no proof
this darn thing works. Each hour we delay
increases risk. Each hour, dozens die,
while Truman, twiddling his thumbs at Potsdam,
waits for word of what we've wrought. I put
my head down, pray, and wait for it.
                                  Now. This.

Philip Morrison

Physicist

Prone on a dike of loose-packed mud,
I curse the rain, the army, my bum leg.

Upwind, off-duty, three SEDs, eager
to witness boom or bust, laugh and bicker.

Giddy as schoolboys skipping class, they wrangle
how best to estimate the fireball.

Drunk on darkness, they stumble, striking sticks
upright at intervals along the dike.

Here at the rim, each half foot extra height
translates at Zero to one thousand feet.

Experiment or spectacle—which stirs
our nonessential but unquestioned presence here?

In the night's flat black, the radio's lit dial
tunes my eyes to twilight's numinous scale.

Tchaikovsky's *Serenade* breaks in, our airwaves
compromised, as Sam intones, "T minus 45."

I don a pair of dime-store shades on which
I've blanked the left lens with a cardboard patch.

One eye for science, but the other's mine.
Only the past is certain. But the future rhymes.

I picture myself half physicist,
half pirate. Both wait on a cannon blast.

"T minus 5." I drop my head. My cheek
hugs chalky soil. The stopwatch stutters, ticks.

Soon history will shout, "Fools" or "Heroes."
Now wind on the dike lip whispers, "Zero."

Edward Teller

Physicist; Super and General Theory Group leader

The seconds limp, then stumble. Stop.
We failed? The thought appalls.
Then zero, and a prick of light.
So faint. Could this be all?

My gloved hands shield the goggles' rim.
Lift one and curtains part.
The scalding sun streams in. Tears blind us.
Triumph. A new start.

Once, young, we feared bad men, the dark.
No more. Today the sun
rose early, on command. I'll learn
to make a bigger one.

Thomas Farrell

Brigadier General, Army Corps of Engineers; Chief of Field Operations

Great poets dream of clarity
and beauty. Even hell
has its finer points. But when
the announcer shouts out, "Now!"
and from the ethereal sky
comes hideous ruin hurled
headlong, flaming, winged
with red lightning and livid
flames' fueled entrails rolling
in black billows, words
are beggared tools for things
that must be seen to be
imagined. "Lord, I believe,"
we all pray—Christian,
Jew, and Atheist—helped
from our unbelief by darkness
shattered and made visible,
the whole great world beyond
our shelter seared by light:
golden, purple, blue, and gray,
more brilliant, many times
the midday sun. The impossible
scientific job is done. Men
step outside to watch the fire
wrapped in shadow, smoking, rise.
The air blast knocks them flat.
Effects that one might once
have called magnificent, stupendous.
Now a wordless, strong,
sustained, and awesome cry
hails Doomsday. Puny,

blasphemous things, we dare
tamper with forces heretofore
reserved to the Almighty.
From the cloisters of physicists'
dreams, an atomic monster
rises as we bid. Seconds
slow. I see with God's
omnipotent eyes. Each peak,
crevasse, and ridge is etched
in flame, and sparrows
drift like sparks across the sky.

Victor Weisskopf

Physicist

I looked at Zero through dark glass. Cloud cloaked
and starless, night stared back. The distant tower
aped a steeple with each lightning stroke.

And then a sun erupted. Stunned, I cowered,
stupid and blind, until the fire dimmed.
An aureole of ions bruised the air,
as though a halo sanctified this star.

A thought—of Grünewald's altarpiece at Colmar:
the Christ ascending in an ochre sphere,
Himself a spike to pierce the night sky's palm.

An awful vision of art clothed in flesh.
The resurrection of a god in wrath.
One thousand billion curies scalding earth.
A forced faith burned into my body's ash.

J. Robert Oppenheimer

Physicist; Director of the Los Alamos Laboratory

After the first flash, white as scalding milk,
blanched eyes dim in their sockets & grope toward
mortal sight, mere fire roiling in charred air.
Wind fists & lifts a cloak of desert dust
in billows & folds shrugged over scarlet
shoulders of flame. A botched shape slowly stands

& roars. Its red breath reeks of burnt sand. Sage
ignites. Birds fall in flames. This is the Song
of God.
          Brow shadows thicken. The figure
rises into thinner air & darkens
& chokes. Its last strangled growlings fatten
an uneasy silence. Some people laugh.

Some cry. I say, "It worked." My tongue is black
with ash. These men have been my many arms.

Once Vishnu tried to teach the prince his duty.
Rising, he roared: Now I am become
Death, the destroyer of worlds.
                    Grant we learn
this time
         before the Red God speaks
                       again.

Joan Hinton

Physicist

The silence lingers longest. Though a new sun
boils above the desert, lifting tons
of dirt and rock-dust miles into the sky,
the burning earth-plume rises without sound.
Even the wind, which had been gusting, stills.
Even the rain that came in quick showers
through the night. Even the lightning
striking the Oscura Mountains.
Even our hearts. Everything stops.
I sit on the cold sand, holding my breath.

David McDonald

Rancher

That morning at my brother's in Adobe,
I woke before the sun was out, thinking
there was a truck backfired, or something like.
I went out on the porch to take a look,
because we wasn't used to strangers then,
despite the goings-on the war had brought
and so forth. Well, I nearly bust a gut,
for there the sun was, rising in the west.
You know, entirely the wrong direction.

Hans Bethe

Head of the Theoretical Division

Nothing like the sun: no CNO
catalysis, no proton-proton chain.
But still our gadget gashes
the grey cloudpack with gold
vermillion and its embers
fall and gall the ground:
fire foretold a billion times

but in the flesh more dangerous.
And lovelier. My heart hides
from its brute beauty, though
only seconds it sputters
bright as an arc electrode
or magnesium flare before

the plume buckles, clouds itself
in silt. Minutes still and dim,
devour a flowering desert
and eclipse the sun's
real rising, reducing rose

to a damasked scent. Baffled
by old dependencies, we minion
to a stunted morning, disciples
of a book that Nature wrote—

a whirling mass of dust
and purple light—our theories,
calculations, measurements correct

to tolerance. War was once a finite
tragedy. We've remade history,

apocalypse a myth no more.

Norris Bradbury

Lt. Commander, US Navy; Physicist

When Trinity went off—
        everybody and his brother
asked me what I thought.
        I'm meant to . . . Hell, I say,
"Thank God the damned thing worked."
        Or words to that effect.

David Nicodemus

Physicist

Dear Mami,
              I am not the same who wrote
you yesterday. The storm has passed. The sun
beats fists against the canvas of my tent
and shakes dust in my eyes with every blow.
I saw a thing last night. I cannot say—
or having said, can't send. You won't know what
a while. But even were I there and free
to talk—I have no words. Or only words.
I don't know what I saw. Frisch said, "A red
hot elephant upended on its trunk."
The other fellows laughed.
                         My rhythm's off.
I saw our village ashed, the men's school burn
again, remembered how the gusting winds
spread pinwheel sparks. The great bass temple bell
on Mukoyama woke us. Cook helped pack
my wicker case. You wedged me in a second
sweater, hid us in the bamboo grove.
We watched while father fought the flames, filling
our honey buckets at the shallow well,
not fast enough. Smoke smudged his preacher's skin
a devil dark—his face a Hannya mask—
as though some jealousy had conjured up
the flames that swallowed almost all he loved.

"Heathens," he might have said, but never did.
He proffered a Trinity, but they preferred
the human godhead of a young marine
biologist. Warlike and practical

and proud, they always had too little faith
in higher powers. Even father's aide,
old Murayama-san, socked all his cash
in dentures, buying gold teeth one by one.
Old samurai, he had the kids pretend
Hirose-gawa was a castle moat
and taught us how to swim with just our feet,
imaginary swords held overhead,
his leather shako leading and, bone dry,
its draggled plume. But father thought he knew
God's will. He spread the Word: "And he rebuked
the winds, and walked upon the waves dry-shod"—
that Christ might be a light to heal blind eyes.

I thought so, too, but planned on getting proof.
A pal and I spent all day laying cable,
sweating our sins away in blazing sun.
Come dusk, we found an empty base camp hut
and stowed our stuff before the storm began.
The roof was tight enough; the instruments
stayed mostly dry. But then brass bullied in.
We packed and grumbled till some GI perched
like a sacred lion on the next hut's steps
shushed us: "The general needs his shut eye." But
we couldn't help the engine being cold.
We gunned it till the crankcase glowed, then beat
a tactical retreat to watch God's will
from a hillside thirty kliks away.
                                    Our friends
were there already, and we sat together
waiting in a deep obscurity
of darkness, like ghosts on a river's brink,
shivering on the damp earth, fearing, longing
to hear the boatman's cry.

                And suddenly
there came a golden heat of sunlight down
and a purple and a royal light shining,
and I knew that God had blessed and damned us,
granting everything that we had wished.

Harriet "Petey" Peterson

Nurse, Los Alamos Hospital

Smitty's smitten, brings me stockings, a few
fresh eggs (won't say from where). How to refuse
his kindnesses? The things I let men do.

I lock the door, hide in Maternity,
but Drs. Love and Large and Stout have keys.
There's no deliverance in Delivery.

Mike breathed sweet barley, bitter hops. Skipped school
to thumb my hem. Thick lipped, my body swooned
and mumbled yes. The things I let men do.

Ghost of a wedding gown, the loose, white johnny
chafed my nipples. Grieving, guilty, I agreed
there's no deliverance in delivery.

Naive and nauseous, seventeen, I knew
what lucky meant. The doctor scraped my womb
clean with a spoon. The things I let men do.

Dilation, curettage. Mistakes, debris.
I learned new words they said would set me free.
But there's no deliverance in delivery.

Now doctors crowd round Oppie, Groves for news.
They celebrate what no one can foresee.
Fat man or thin, the things we let them do.
There's no deliverance in delivery.

David McDonald

Rancher

And it was quite a while, y'know, till they
begin to talk about the cattle—how
their hair was turning white on them, like frost.
The way we noticed it was if a cow
was lying on her left side, well her right
would get a burn from particles of fallout
falling there, causing a burn just like a scald,
and then the hair, instead of growing red
like on a Hereford cow, would come back white,
the way a saddle burn shows on a black horse.
And old Mack Smith, as owns the general store,
had a cat just as black as the ace of spades,
till that thing grew white spots all over it.
He sold it to some tourist, for five dollars
I think it was, as a curiosity.

Joe Willis

Projectionist, Loma Theater

We'd wished for miracles, of course. A son
  of David come to heal her sight,
a sainted Einstein of the eyes, even
  a local doc whose homegrown insight
might set her damaged retina to rights.
  Despite our prayers, this wasn't that.
Which didn't stop the *Chieftain* making hay
  from hearsay, once the army dropped
its guard, and "Ammunition Dump Explodes"
  became "Socorro Blind Girl Sees
Atomic Bomb." It sold some papers, fooled
  a lot of people. Mostly fools.
The way they stamped on facts and feelings burned
  me up, but Georgia only laughed.
"They want a myth. Why interview mere flesh
  and blood? I fit their letter, though
I'm something shy in spirit." Shy's ten miles
  from how I'd put it. Georgia's been
a candle in the window these years since
  I 'came her kin. Her radiance
is worth folks staring at, but all they see's
  her dead glass eye, the other drifting
like a B-flick fortune-teller oohing
  and aahing over cold tea dregs.
They pity her for all that she can't see,
  and then they're scared of what she can.

Els thinks her sister's life is like a movie
  when the film stock snags and burns and been
that way since she turned seven and she gouged
  her good eye on the ice box door.

The other eye, though—Els clams up and claims
    she was too young and can't recall.
To hear Lucina tell it, seems she thinks
    Georgia was touched by God at birth:
one pupil huge in wide-eyed wonderment,
    as if a world that beautiful
could only but be swallowed whole. She says
    her daughter did a lifetime's worth
of seeing in her first three years, despite
    her bad eye bloating like a slow
explosion till the doctors had no choice
    but yank it out before it burst.

Georgia's not one to bellyache. She likes
    to sit, spine stiff as chimney stone,
and let her fingers natter at some task,
    fast as the flick of coachwhip tongues.
She learns things' outlines off by heart, palming
    her mother's knickknacks like a birth-
day conjuror, her gestures echoing
    the world. She likes bright spots or dark
best, places most folks shy from, peeling spuds
    in the root cellar's clammy gloom
or shucking corn with her back to the sun-
    kilned kitchen wall. She tilts her head
like a flower following the blaze. At sunset
    she sits out back, brandishing
her father's squawk box like a dusty fryer
    she can pluck in half the time Els takes.
She stares up at the sky. Her fingers fly.
    I close my eyes and swear someone
put on a brand-new disc of Jean Vaissade.

    But when she hums and mumbles day
long with no melody in sight, I'm fit

to truss. Els says her music is
a gift she gets from living in the dark,
    but this is something else—a sound
track, maybe, or magician's patter meant
    to blind us to some trick. She says
the world is poorly drawn; she sings to press
    things back into their proper shapes.
She offers chickens, oranges, a chair.
    I say I hear the differences.
She doesn't call me what I am. Light drowns
    the ears, she says. Some days I punch
in early at the Loma, choose a seat,
    lights out, in back, and listen hard.

But Georgia likes front rows. Most Saturdays
    she tags along, sits through the show,
head tipped up toward the flashing screen. That week
    brought Bogart's *Conflict*, pale beside
Fox Movietone's first Kamikaze clips:
    the *Bunker Hill* hit hard, its flight
deck an inferno, men awash in flames.
    I asked her later what she saw.
Blotches of dark and light, she said. A war.

    It rained that night. I woke with dawn
two hours off, the tang of creosote
    musting the still-damp dark. I shaved,
thinking of flowers summer downpours kindle,
    the desert pricked with little suns.
I lit the kitchen lamp. Georgia was up
    already, as she always is,
a book spread open on her knees. She stroked
    the pages like you would a cat.
She'd propped the back door open, dragged her chair
    beside it. Darkness rubbed its flank

against the door frame. Els fried eggs. I boiled
    the coffee. As we ate, a breeze
drew off the river, sweet with cottonwood.
    The birds began their tuning up,
and Georgia whistled like a thrush, then tapped
    her fingers, mimicking the storm's
spent rhythm. Els roused us. "Our college girl's
    due back at school. Rehearsal starts
at seven." Georgia packed her instrument,
    a stack of scores to share with friends,
riddled with quavers she will never see.
    Els squeezed in back with Georgia's case,
hoping that Kistler's might have nylons stocked.

    The sky spread out above us, taut
and blank as a darkened screen. The road unspooled
    and Georgia hummed. The car hummed, too.
And then, a mile past Lemitar, and suddenly
    a Peerless carbon arc ignites,
and Georgia says, "What's that?" and history
    is made because a blind girl saw—
What? Revelation? God's descent in wrath?
    I couldn't keep us straight. I hit
the brakes and swerved and skidded off the road.
    Georgia was quickest getting out.
She stood with one hand on the car's warm hood.
    We joined her in unearthly light.
Els echoed, "Joe, what is that?" Who could say?
    I might have sworn it was the sun,
except it didn't crest the eastern hills
    by inches like a glass filled past
the brim, but burst—a flood of scalding light
    across the desert south of us.
If God is light, it was a kind of midnight:
    something no one's meant to see.

It should have scotched what little sight we had.
   Instead, we all stood, tranced—like kids
staring in first-time movie wonder—stunned
   by cloudy curtains parting, gilt-
edged billowings and purple flowing folds
   framing a balled flame rising, scarlet,
puckered, slowly fading with the dull, sick sheen
   of sideshow pyrotechnics.
                                        Silence,
then the sudden brawl of thunder gusting north.
   The ground shook some. I thought to breathe.
I handed Georgia back into the car.
   We drove on through returning night.
The headlamps groped ahead, imagining
   the road for me. She didn't hum.

What sorry bastard wouldn't see himself
   in her? Who wouldn't pray that God
will give her sight—a sign that anyone
   might rise out of this stubborn dark?
But now these heathen scientists, these lab-
   bound moles, have learned to imitate
the dawn. They nose stale crumbs of earth, project
   our own pale shadows on blank stone.
Maybe the army censors got it right.
   Some things are only ever lies.
Better to ask a blind girl what she saw.
   Best to be spared such miracles.

Edith Warner

Ran a tearoom by the Rio Grande

As season follows season, I sense a change,
though subtle, in the earth. Like the thin veil of green
that mantles the desert after rain, a change
has come upon the land. Or else, I hope, the difference is in me.
Now when I smell the Russian olive's bloom each May,
when the woods along the river fill with its rosy scent,
another odor teases my palate, faint, vague, but inescapable—
like the hint of bitterness in milk that will soon sour.
Now when I hear wind in the salt cedar's feathery leaves,
another sound frets gently in my ear, almost inaudible,
like the whispered passing of a rattlesnake across dry sand.
And now when I see children in the pueblo spreading sheets
beneath the piñon trees to gather nuts, high on the edge of sight
a brief metallic glint catches my eye, then vanishes,
and I stop, and the veil falls, and I listen for the bee drone
fading in and out on the drifting wind. And if
I have not heard it yet, I know, I can't forget, I might.

J. Robert Oppenheimer

Physicist; Director of the Los Alamos Laboratory

We lost the moon among mountains,
urging our horses forward, watching ribbons
of steam rise from their flanks as they climbed in the midnight cold.
We had left the trail. Crisis's steel shoes sang
on the sandstone outcrops. High slopes
barred the sky.

The moon was waiting down by the river
where the boatman slept in an old alder shack
between two palms. We pulled ourselves
across the wrinkled water. Slick, moon-silvered planks echoed
when our horses stamped. The wet ropes
chafed our hands.

On the far bank, soaptrees bloomed, pale, odorless.
We called farewell to the sleeping boatman. The salty breath
of desert tamarisks replied
as the moon set behind Los Alamos.
Their dry leaves flickered like candles
and went out.

Acknowledgments

While writing this book I received crucial support in the form of fellowships from the Watson Foundation, the Vermont Studio Center, Rutgers University, Boston University, and the Massachusetts Cultural Council.

My thanks to the editors of the following publications, in which many of these poems first appeared, often in different form:

> *At Length, The Beloit Poetry Journal, The Bulletin of the Atomic Scientists, The Cincinnati Review, Cordite Poetry Review, The Gettysburg Review, Grist, Harvard Divinity Bulletin, The Hudson Review, LIT, New England Review, The New Republic, Poetry Daily, Prairie Schooner, Raritan, Salamander, Solstice, The Southern Review, The Southwest Review, Slate, The Virginia Quarterly Review.*

And to the editors of these anthologies:

> *The Autumn House Anthology of Poetry*, ed. Sue Ellen Thompson (Autumn House Press, 2005); *A Face to Meet the Faces: Persona Poems*, ed. Stacey Lynn Brown and Oliver de la Paz (University of Akron Press, 2012); *Filling the Hole in the Nuclear Future: Art and Popular Culture in Response to the Atomic Bomb in the US and Japan*, ed. Robert Jacobs (Hiroshima Peace Institute and Rowman & Littlefield, 2010); *Nuclear Impact: Broken Atoms in Our Hands*, ed. Teresa Mei Chuc (Shabda Press, 2017); *Poetry Daily Essentials 2007*, ed. Diane Boller and Don Selby (Sourcebooks, 2007); *Salamander: 10th Anniversary Anthology*, ed. Jennifer Barber and Jacquelyn Pope (Salamander, 2003/2004).

Thanks also to the archivists and staff of the Los Alamos National Labora-
tory, the Los Alamos Historical Society, the Niels Bohr Library of the Ameri-
can Institute of Physics, the Oregon State University Libraries Special Collec-
tions and Archives Research Center, the National Archives and Records
Administration, and the Archive of the Niels Bohr Institute at the University
of Copenhagen.

Special thanks to the Manhattan Project participants and their families who
shared memories and perceptions with me: Norris Bradbury, William and
Beebe Caldes, Winston Dabney, Rachel Fermi, Kenneth Greisen, Sigmund and
Florence Harris, William Higginbotham, Fred House, Theodore Jorgensen,
Joanna Jorgensen Kaestner, Stephen Marshak, Joseph McKibben, John Mench,
William Menker, Philip Morrison, Robert Porton, Glenn Price, Joan Bain-
bridge Safford, Raemer Schreiber, Florence and Ben Schulkin, Robert Serber,
William Spindel, Meyer Steinberg, James and Sally Taub, Edward Teller, Rudy
Vergoth, Robert Webster, Jay Wechsler, John Weil, Victor Weisskopf, John
Wieneke, and Robert Wilson. Lloyd Garrison, Robert Oppenheimer's lawyer
during his security clearance hearing in 1954, also graciously shared his experi-
ences and observations with me.

Friends and colleagues offered encouragement, guidance, and inspiration:
Agha Shahid Ali, Tony Arefin, Rick Benjamin, Ben Berman, Olga Broumas,
Catherine Corman, Tom Daley, Stephen Donadio, Elsa Dorfman, Dan and
Andrea Elish, Jon Else, Chris Gavaler, Pamela White Hadas, Geoffrey Hill,
John Hollander, Mark Jarman, Myra Jehlen, Donald Justice, Jennie Kiffmeyer,
Galway Kinnell, Sydney Lea, Lisa Lee, Brad Leithauser, George Levine, Paul
Mariani, William Matthews, Wendy McDowell, Joshua Mehigan, Lenore
Myers, David Narlee, Talia Neffson, Howard Nemerov, Tim O'Brien, Sherry
Ortner, Robert Pack, Jay Parini, Linda Pastan, Omar Pound, Rosamond Pur-
cell, Shoshana Razel, Justin Rosenberg, Alan Shapiro, William Stafford, Ruth
Stone, Mark Strand, Ted Sutton, Tim Taylor, Lisa Verploegh, Lesley Wheeler,
and Marian Yee.

Above and beyond gratitude to Daniel Bosch, Richard Kenney, and Derek
Walcott.

John Coster-Mullen, X. J. Kennedy, Errol Morris, Richard Rhodes, and Martin Sherwin generously read this manuscript when it dropped on them out of the blue. Any remaining inaccuracies or inconsistencies are mine (or history's).

Family supported me through the long haul. The deepest thanks of hand in glove go to Betsy, Tom, Matthew, Melissa, Leslie, Rudd and Jerry.

Notes on Poems

Individuals cited in *italic type* in these notes are also represented by their own poems, and more information about them may be found in those poems and in the "Biographical Notes" section at the end of this volume.

Epigraphs

Auden: from "The Poet & The City" in *The Dyer's Hand*.
Sacks: from *The Man Who Mistook His Wife for a Hat*.

Poems

William Laurence (1)

Farrell: Brigadier General *Thomas Farrell* of the Army Corps of Engineers was Chief of Field Operations for the Manhattan Project and Leslie Groves's second-in-command.

Groves: Brigadier General *Leslie Groves* of the Army Corps of Engineers was the military head of the Manhattan Project.

Once our sun has risen: The Japanese name for Japan (Nippon or Nihon) means "the sun's origin" and is often translated as "the Land of the Rising Sun."

Albert Einstein (5)

Peconic Bay: two heavily sheltered bays at the eastern end of Long Island where Einstein rented a summer house and sailed his boat, *Tinef*.

Nostra culpa: Latin for "our guilt."

Leo Szilard (6)

Rutherford: Lord Ernest Rutherford, an experimental physicist and director of the Cavendish Laboratory at Cambridge University.

Otto Mandl: Viennese timber merchant and husband of pianist Lili Krauss, who
lived in London and on whom Szilard relied for meals almost daily.

Soddy's book on radium: Wells's dedication reads: "To Frederick Soddy's
Interpretation of Radium this story, which owes long passages to the eleventh
chapter of that book, acknowledges and inscribes itself." Soddy was an
English radiochemist who, in collaboration with Rutherford, determined
that radioactivity involves the old alchemical dream of the transmutation of
elements.

Archimedes dreaming Hiero's crown: Archimedes, a Greek mathematician and
scientist, was asked by King Hiero to determine whether a crown he had
commissioned was pure gold. To do this, Archimedes needed to find a way to
determine the crown's volume without melting it down. While lying in a bath,
he realized that immersed objects displace an equal volume of water. He was
so excited that he leapt up without dressing and ran through the streets yelling,
"Eureka!" ("I have found it!").

Eugene Wigner (8)

Our decade's-old conversion: Wigner's family converted from Judaism to
Lutheranism to avoid persecution in the wake of Béla Kun's short-lived
communist regime in Hungary in 1919.

hausfrau: German for "housewife."

Otto Frisch (9)

Kernphysik: German for "nuclear physics."

zu jüdisch: German for "too Jewish."

Stern shilled my resume: Otto Stern, who would win the Nobel Prize in Physics
in 1943, was Frisch's boss at the University of Hamburg. Stern also left the
university when Hitler came into power in 1933.

Blackett: When Frisch left Hamburg, he went to work for P. M. S. Blackett, a
British experimental physicist at Birkbeck College in London.

Aunt Lise: Lise Meitner and Otto Hahn were joint heads of the Department of
Radioactivity Research at the Kaiser Wilhelm Institute for Chemistry in
Berlin. After thirty years of collaboration with Hahn, at the age of sixty, she
was forced to flee Nazi Germany in 1938, just before identifying the results of
their bombardment of uranium with neutrons.

Anschluss: German for "connection," the term used by the Nazis to describe their
annexation of Austria in 1938.

God Himself: *Niels Bohr*, a Danish physicist, Director of the Institute of
   Theoretical Physics at the University of Copenhagen, and winner of the
   Nobel Prize in Physics in 1922.
Dad interned in Dachau: Frisch eventually managed to obtain a passport for his
   father and permission for him to travel to Sweden.

Max Delbruck (11)
E equals M times C quadrat: $E = mc^2$.
Chadwick's gaze: Sir James Chadwick, the English experimental physicist who
   discovered the neutron (a neutral particle that contributes mass to atoms)
   and served as Rutherford's assistant director of research at the Cavendish
   Laboratory.
Pauli's intellect: Wolfgang Pauli, a prominent theoretical physicist from Austria,
   taught at Princeton during the war.
Heisenberg: Werner Heisenberg, a German theoretical physicist and pioneer of
   quantum mechanics who developed the uncertainty principle in 1927. During
   World War II, he served as one of the chief physicists in Germany's nuclear
   weapons program.
Schrödinger: Erwin Schrödinger, an Austrian theoretical physicist and a principal
   contributor to the development of quantum mechanics.
uncertainty: Heisenberg's uncertainty principle states that there is always a
   degree of imprecision (uncertainty) in our measurements of the momentum
   and position of a particle—the more accurately one is measured, the less
   precisely the other can be known.
Ehrenfest: Paul Ehrenfest, a Dutch and Austrian theoretical physicist who made
   important contributions to the development of quantum mechanics. After
   struggling with depression ("DESPERATION"), he committed suicide.
Strahlungstheorie: German for "radiation theory."
$\Psi\Psi^*$: The Greek letter Ψ (psi) represents a wave function describing the quantum
   state of a system; Ψ^* (psi star) represents the complex conjugate of the wave
   function, having an identical real portion and an imaginary portion that has
   equal magnitude but the opposite sign. Here they are multiplied together,
   yielding a result with no imaginary part.
infinite self-energy: The energy required to assemble a particle ("self-energy") is
   theoretically infinite.
Weisskopf: *Victor Weisskopf*, an Austrian physicist who later served as a group
   leader in the Theoretical Division at Los Alamos.

Otto Frisch (15)

Fermi: Enrico Fermi, an Italian theoretical physicist who won the Nobel Prize in
Physics in 1938. During the war, he oversaw construction of a uranium pile
(under the stands of Stagg Field at the University of Chicago) that produced
the first man-made nuclear chain reaction. In 1944 he moved to Los Alamos
as associate director of the laboratory.

Hahn and Strassmann: Otto Hahn and Fritz Strassmann were German chemists
who, with Frisch's aunt, Lise Meitner, performed experiments in which they
bombarded uranium with neutrons.

Joliot-Curie: The husband and wife team of Irène Curie and Jean Frédéric Joliot
shared the Nobel Prize in Chemistry in 1935 for their discovery of artificial
radioactivity. Irène died of leukemia that may have been the result of her
work with radioactive substances. (Most references to Irène and Frédéric
identify them with a hyphenated surname, Joliot-Curie, but in their scientific
publications they retained their original single surnames.)

my chamber: A cloud chamber is a sealed container supersaturated with water
or alcohol vapor used to detect charged particles such as alpha or beta
radiation.

Lise: Lise Meitner, Frisch's aunt, had recently fled Nazi Germany, abandoning
her position as joint head (with Otto Hahn) of the Department of
Radioactivity Research at the Kaiser Wilhelm Institute for Chemistry.

Otto's note: the letter from Hahn to Meitner reporting that the neutron
bombardment of uranium had produced barium.

the body's tagged: When Meitner fled Berlin, she left behind a sample produced
by the bombardment of uranium with neutrons. She did not have an
opportunity to analyze the sample, but Hahn subsequently identified it as
barium. He was awarded the Nobel Prize in Chemistry in 1944; Meitner was
overlooked.

Kungälv: A small city north of Gothenburg in Sweden.

Göta älv: The "River of the Geats" that flows from Lake Vänern to the North Sea
on the west coast of Sweden.

Gamow: George Gamow, a Russian theoretical physicist and cosmologist who
defected from the Soviet Union and became an US citizen in 1940.

Schrödinger: Erwin Schrödinger, an Austrian theoretical physicist and a principal
contributor to the development of quantum mechanics.

Bohr: *Niels Bohr*, a Danish physicist, Director of the Institute of Theoretical
Physics at the University of Copenhagen, and winner of the Nobel Prize in
Physics in 1922.

Nature and *Naturwissenschaften*: Leading scientific journals.

our chamber groups: Frisch, an accomplished pianist, participated in musical chamber groups and collaborated with other scientists in cloud chamber experiments.

Leo Szilard (18)

Wigner: *Eugene Wigner*, a Hungarian theoretical physicist and mathematician who shared the Nobel Prize in Physics in 1963. He was known to friends as Wigwam.

King's Crown: The King's Crown Hotel, 420 West 116th Street, in New York City. Wigner and Szilard visited Einstein on July 12, 1939.

"Daran habe ich gar nicht gedacht": "That I did not think."

Albert Einstein (19)

induction flow refrigerators: In response to deaths caused by leaky refrigerator pumps, *Leo Szilard* convinced Einstein to collaborate on the design of a safer refrigerator with no moving parts.

Edward Teller (20)

Punkts and *Kommas*: German for "periods" and "commas."

Thales: A machine for performing mathematical calculations.

Albert Einstein (26)

Tinef: The name of Einstein's fifteen-foot sailboat, from the Western European Yiddish word for "junk." Einstein was apparently a poor but enthusiastic sailor.

Helen: Helen Dukas, Einstein's secretary.

Unified Field Theory: A theory uniting two or more of the four fundamental forces (gravity, electromagnetism, and the strong and weak nuclear forces) in a single conceptual scheme. Einstein's quest was, in particular, to reconcile the general theory of relativity (which addresses gravity) with electromagnetism.

Alexander Sachs (31)

Fulton: Robert Fulton, an American engineer and steamboat inventor, was commissioned by Napoleon Bonaparte to design the first submarine; Fulton then offered to build "the Little Corporal" a fleet of steam-powered naval vessels.

Leslie Groves (34)

My Buddha: Groves's nickname for his wife, Grace.

Somervell: Lieutenant General Brehon Burke Somervell commanded the Army Service Forces, which included the Army Corps of Engineers.

Styer: Major General Wilhelm Styer was Somervell's chief of staff.

Bugle Notes: the *Handbook of the United States Corps of Cadets*, also known as "the West Point Plebe Bible."

Old Pot: Colonel Ernest Graves, a mentor to Groves.

Robert Serber (38)

Oppie: *J. Robert Oppenheimer*, Serber's physics professor at the University of California, Berkeley; later director of the Los Alamos Laboratory, where the first nuclear weapons were designed and built.

Perro Caliente: "Hot dog!"

Katie Page: Katherine Chaves Page, wife of an older Chicago businessman, ran Los Pinos, a dude ranch north of Santa Fe. Oppenheimer first met her when he was still a teenager; she taught him to ride, and after he got over his crush on her, they became lifelong friends.

Charlotte: Serber's wife; she would run the technical library at the Los Alamos laboratory.

John Dudley (41)

Shangri-La: the paradisiacal valley in James Hilton's 1933 novel, *Lost Horizon*.

Edith Warner (43)

Connell: Albert James "A.J." Connell, director of the Los Alamos Ranch School, which the army would commandeer and turn into a nuclear weapons laboratory in 1943.

Louis Slotin (46)

Bethe: *Hans Bethe*, a German physicist, head of the Theoretical Division at Los Alamos.

Bloch: Felix Bloch, a Swiss experimental physicist.

Bohr: *Niels Bohr*, a Danish physicist and director of the Institute of Theoretical Physics at the University of Copenhagen, fled the Nazi occupation and served as a visiting consultant at Los Alamos.

Dorothy McKibben (48)

Lost Almosts: A nickname for residents of the Los Alamos laboratory.

Robert Serber (50)

The portions of this poem in quotes are a collage of Serber's own words as recorded in *The Los Alamos Primer*, edited by Richard Rhodes (see Sources).

Richard Feynman (52)

Arline: Feynman's wife.

Edward Condon (54)

Lewis: As a graduate student, Condon started his dissertation under E. P. Lewis, an experimental physicist and chair of Berkeley's physics department.

apples split for pickling, or boiled eggs divided by a hair: In Plato's *Symposium*, Aristophanes describes an original "third sex" of humanity—a union of male and female—which, in its strength and pride, attempted to scale heaven. The apple and egg metaphors describe the gods' response: division of the united sexes into separate halves that eternally longed for one another.

Tizard's magnetron: Sir Henry Thomas Tizard, an English chemist and inventor, led a mission to the United States in 1940 to share information about British scientific advances, including the magnetron, a microwave generator.

Rabi: Isidor Isaac Rabi, an American physicist and friend of *J. Robert Oppenheimer*'s, worked on radar at MIT during World War II and served as a consultant at Los Alamos.

N-dimensional mess space: from Edward U. Condon, "Food and the Theory of Probability," *United States Naval Institute Proceedings*, 60:1 (January 1934), pp. 75–8.

Wilson's "thousand twangling instruments": Robert Rathbun Wilson, an American experimental physicist and sculptor, was the Cyclotron Group leader at Los Alamos. A cyclotron is a large machine that uses magnetic and electric fields to accelerate atomic and subatomic particles.

Alamogordo: a small town in southern New Mexico, just east of the Trinity site where the first nuclear bomb was tested on July 16, 1945.

Emilie: Condon's wife.

Mädi: Condon's daughter.

Louis Slotin (58)

Okhrana: Russian for "security"; an abbreviation for the Department for Protecting the Public Security and Order, the secret police of Imperial Russia.

Protocols: The Protocols of the Elders of Zion, a text supposedly written by Jews describing their plan for world domination but actually invented by the Okhrana and used by anti-Semitic groups across the globe to justify persecution of Jewish populations.

Белая Русь: Belaya Rus, "White Russia," the eastern portion of the Republic of Belarus.

Отец: Otyets, "father."

Morgan: Kyle Morgan, an American physicist at the Oak Ridge, Tennessee, branch of the Manhattan Project.

BVDs: a brand of underwear.

Peer de Silva (60)

G-2: the US Army Military Intelligence Corps.

Edward Teller (62)

Wigwam: *Eugene Wigner*, a Hungarian theoretical physicist and mathematician.

Tegernsee: a mountainous region near the town and lake of the same name in Bavaria.

Von Lossow: the German surgeon who operated on Teller after he lost his foot, using a procedure developed by a Russian surgeon, Nikolay Ivanovich Pirogov, in which Teller's fibula and tibia were fused to the remaining part of his heel. The result required a bulkier prosthesis but allowed Teller to bear weight on his stump.

Ruth Marshak (63)

candle every egg: Holding an egg in front of a candle allows one to see whether a fetus has begun to develop.

James Nolan (64)

G-men: agents of G-2, the US Army's Military Intelligence Corps.

Weisskopf: *Victor Weisskopf*, an Austrian physicist who served as a group leader in the Theoretical Division at Los Alamos.

John Dudley (65)

Ashbridge: Colonel Whitney Ashbridge served as Commander of the Los Alamos
  Army Post from the spring of 1943 to the fall of 1944. He was, coincidentally,
  a graduate of the Los Alamos Ranch School.

La Fonda: a hotel and bar in Santa Fe.

Bernice Brode (67)

Mary: Mary Frankel was Brode's immediate "overseer." She had degrees in
  both mathematics and psychology and had worked in the latter field before
  joining the scientific staff at Los Alamos. Her husband was the theoretical
  physicist Stanley Frankel.

Marchant: a mechanical calculator made by the Marchant Calculating Machine
  Company.

Mici: Mici Teller, wife of theoretical physicist *Edward Teller*.

Moll Flanders: The mathematician Donald "Moll" Flanders led the Computations
  Group in the Theoretical Division and founded the Los Alamos Choral
  Society.

Joe: Joseph Hirschfelder trained the computers, usually wives of scientists, who
  did not have scientific backgrounds. He had doctorates in both physics and
  chemistry and was the Interior Ballistics Group leader in the Ordnance
  and Engineering Division at Los Alamos. Hirschfelder had received
  permission to bring his mother with him to Los Alamos; "Ma," as she was
  affectionately known to her neighbors, had no official responsibilities but
  cooked and cleaned for her son and threw herself wholeheartedly into life
  on the Mesa.

Edward Teller (69)

Bethe: *Hans Bethe*, a German physicist, head of the Theoretical Division at Los
  Alamos. Teller believed he deserved the position.

stopped by the hospital: Bethe visited Teller while he was in the hospital
  recovering from the loss of his foot in a tram accident.

the endless clanking gears: See Teller's first poem, "Now Einstein knows me . . ."

Gives me a group: Oppenheimer created the Super and General Theory Group
  largely to placate Teller, even though work on the Super (the hydrogen
  bomb) was, in Teller's own words, "beyond the immediate aims of the
  laboratory."

Klaus Fuchs (70)

Christel: Fuchs's younger sister.

Elisabeth: Fuchs's older sister, who committed suicide by throwing herself in front of a train to escape arrest for communist activities.

Tauschwert: German for "exchange value," which Karl Marx distinguished from "use value."

Gerhard: Fuchs's older brother.

Hans Staub: a childhood acquaintance.

her job was done: Fuchs's mother, Else, committed suicide by drinking hydrochloric acid.

Eugene Wigner (74)

Belcza-Puszta: Wigner's uncle had an estate in Belcza-Puszta in southern Hungary near the Danube.

Amelia: Amelia Frank, a physics student at the University of Wisconsin, where Wigner taught.

Edith Warner (76)

Lattimore: Richmond Lattimore, an American translator of Homer's *Iliad* and *Odyssey*.

Tilano: Atilano Montoya, former governor of the San Ildefonso Pueblo and uncle of potter Maria Martinez (see *Antonio Martinez*), first came to Edith's house circa 1928 to build her a fireplace; he stayed with her to recover from a drinking binge, became a teetotaler, and ended up living with Edith for the rest of his life. The nature of the relationship remained mysterious, even to those who knew them well: Tilano was a generation older than Edith, but she demonstrated a distinctly maternal care for him. Their relationship has been described both as a beautiful friendship and as a great love story.

Niels Bohr: the Danish Nobel laureate in physics.

Bethes, Fermis, Allisons, and *Tellers*: Los Alamos scientists and their families.

Peter's diabolical contraption: A typewriter given to Edith by her goddaughter, Peter Miller.

Brownie: Tilano's nephew would be on the aircraft carrier USS *Bunker Hill* when it was hit by two kamikaze planes at Okinawa (see *Joe Willis*). He survived.

hunt system: Edith was a poor typist and had to "hunt and peck" each letter.

Kitty: *Kitty Oppenheimer*, wife of Robert, the scientific director of Los Alamos.

Pronto: Kitty's son Peter, called Pronto because he was born seven months after she married Oppie.

Compton, Tuck, and Segre: Los Alamos scientists.

J. Robert Oppenheimer (78)

Jean's gone: Between 1936 and 1939, Jean Tatlock had been Oppenheimer's on-again, off-again lover—twice "close enough to marriage to think of ourselves as engaged," in Oppenheimer's words—before he married Kitty. Tatlock was a psychiatrist and physician at Mount Zion Hospital, now part of the University of California, San Francisco Medical Center, when in June 1943, while on a recruiting trip from Los Alamos, Oppenheimer spent the night with her, later explaining the visit by saying, "She had indicated a great desire to see me. . . . She was undergoing psychiatric treatment. She was extremely unhappy." G-2 security officers recorded the visit, which later gave Oppenheimer's enemies ammunition in their efforts to strip him of his security clearance after the war. In early January 1944, Tatlock drowned in her bathtub. According to the coroner's report, there were barbiturates and "a faint trace of chloral hydrate" (the active ingredient in a "Mickey Finn") in her system. Although she left a suicide note, oddities in her death have led some people to speculate that she might have been killed, perhaps even by G-2 agents.

Bohr: *Niels Bohr*, the eminent physicist, acted as a visiting consultant at Los Alamos.

"Be this my text": from John Donne, "Hymn to God, My God, in My Sickness."

"Trip no further": from William Shakespeare, *Twelfth Night*, act 2, scene 3.

"I mount the stairs": from T. S. Eliot, "Portrait of a Lady."

Corti: a commune (township) on the island of Corsica. In March 1926, while Oppenheimer was a graduate student at Cambridge University, he and three friends bicycled across the island.

Le Recherché: *À la recherche du temps perdu* is a seven-volume novel by Marcel Proust (translated as *In Search of Lost Time* or *Remembrance of Things Past*), which Oppenheimer read on Corsica. The following lines are from the first volume, *Du côté de chez Swann* (*Swann's Way*): "indifférence aux souffrances qu'on cause . . . est la forme terrible et permanente de la cruauté."

Stenosis: When Oppenheimer was four, his mother gave birth to a boy (Lewis Frank Oppenheimer) who died shortly after of stenosis of the pylorus—a

narrowing of the passage between the stomach and small intestine due to
swelling of the pyloric valve.

Abbot's Nembutal: A bottle of Abbot's Nembutal C, a sleeping drug, was found
in Tatlock's apartment with only two tablets left.

Truchas Peak divide: four summits comprising a single massif in the Sangre
de Cristo Mountains on the divide between the Rio Grande and the Pecos
River.

Kitty Oppenheimer (80)

Marshal Keitel: Wilhelm Keitel, Hitler's head of the Oberkommando der
Wehrmacht (High Command of the German Armed Forces).

James Nolan (81)

Petey: *Harriet "Petey" Peterson* worked as a nurse at the Los Alamos base hospital.

Gigi: GG for "General Groves," a common nickname for *Leslie Groves*.

Robert Serber (83)

T-Division: the Theoretical Division at Los Alamos.

Manley: John Manley, an American physicist and one of Oppenheimer's closest
aids at Los Alamos, brought the Cockcroft-Walton generator, used as a
particle accelerator, to Los Alamos from the University of Illinois at Urbana–
Champaign.

Bob Wilson: Robert Rathbun Wilson led the Cyclotron Group at Los Alamos.

Priscilla: Priscilla Duffield served as Robert Oppenheimer's secretary at Los
Alamos.

Dumbarton Oaks: a historic estate in Georgetown, owned by Harvard University
and used during August, September, and October of 1944 as the site of an
international conference establishing the United Nations.

Willy Higinbotham (85)

Karloff: Boris Karloff played the monster in the 1931 film *Frankenstein*.

Fritz: Dr. Henry Frankenstein's hunchbacked assistant (the precursor of Igor).
The character does not appear in the novel by Mary Shelley; he is killed by
the monster after tormenting it with a torch and a whip.

stomach Steinway: an accordion.

Strickfaden: Kenneth Strickfaden was an electrician who designed special effects
(often using Tesla coils) for movies ranging from the original *Frankenstein* to
Mel Brook's 1974 *Young Frankenstein*.

Edith Warner (87)

tombé: a double-headed Native American drum.

Niels Bohr (88)

twinned fields: Electromagnetic radiation (such as visible light) consists of
   alternating oscillations of electric and magnetic fields.

Tom Mix: a prolific American movie actor who starred in Westerns between 1909
   and 1935.

Schrödinger's boxed cat: a thought experiment devised by Erwin Schrödinger,
   an Austrian physicist, in 1935 in which a cat is placed in a steel chamber
   with a tiny sample of a radioactive substance and a flask of hydrogen
   cyanide that will break if one of the radioactive atoms decays (with a 50
   percent probability that an atom will decay in the course of an hour).
   Schrödinger called the experiment "ridiculous" but argued that it illustrated
   the "entanglement" of the macroscopic cat with the indeterminacy of the
   atomic domain and that until it was opened the box would contain both a
   living and a dead cat in equal parts.

a wobbly lush between policemen: The squeeze theorem in calculus compares
   the limit of a function to those of two other functions between which it
   is "sandwiched," "pinched," or "squeezed." It is also known as the "two
   policemen and a drunk theorem": if two policemen usher a drunkard
   between them, and both policemen end up at the police station, then
   the drunkard must end up at the station as well, no matter how much he
   staggers along the way.

selbst: German for "self."

Baker: Bohr's Manhattan Project codename was "Nicholas Baker," which led to
   the affectionate "nickname" of Uncle Nick.

the pope: Enrico Fermi, the Italian theoretical physicist who served as associate
   director of Los Alamos, was known as "the pope" because of his infallibility.

God has diced: *Einstein* and Bohr had a running debate about the implications of
   quantum theory: Bohr maintained that the theory's probabilistic description
   reflected the character of nature itself, while Einstein believed that the
   theory was only a stopgap on the way to a causal description, expressing
   his belief most famously in a 1926 letter to the German physicist Max Born,
   "Der Alte nicht würfelt" ("The old man [God] does not play dice").

Dorothy McKibben (94)

Joe: McKibben's husband died of Hodgkin's lymphoma in 1931.

Havasu: Havasu Falls in the Grand Canyon. McKibben was camping there with her friends Eliot Porter (the photographer), Aline Porter (his wife), and Cady Wells (the painter) when the Nazis invaded Holland in May 1940.

Antonio Martinez (96)

San Ildefonso: a pueblo in New Mexico, northwest of Santa Fe and east of Los Alamos.

Mother: Maria Martinez, an internationally known Native American potter.

Hans Bethe: head of the Theoretical Division at Los Alamos.

RaLa: An experiment using radioactive lanthanum to study the compression of plutonium in response to converging shock waves during the implosion process.

Omega: Omega site was an isolated part of the Los Alamos laboratory where some of the more dangerous experiments, such as the Water Boiler reactor, were conducted.

clay slips: slurries of clay and other materials as needed by the potter.

kajepes: tools cut from gourds to smooth and shape clay pots.

the red fox, luck: Martinez's Tewa name, Popovi Da, translates as "Red Fox."

the Van de Graaff: a generator that uses a moving belt to create large voltages.

Chien-Shiung Wu (100)

Wigner: the Hungarian physicist *Eugene Wigner*.

B Pile: the world's first full-scale uranium reactor, constructed at the Hanford, Washington, branch of the Manhattan Project. It came online in September 1944 and was used to "breed" plutonium for the Trinity and Nagasaki bombs.

Fermi: The Italian physicist Enrico Fermi designed the first uranium reactor (at the University of Chicago) and then oversaw construction of large scale versions at Hanford.

daughter fission products: When the atoms of a substance "fish" (fission), they split into less massive elements known as "daughter products."

Parity: Wu's experimental work would, in 1956, confirm the invalidity of the principle of conservation of parity (the idea that left- and right-handed components of particles participate with equal frequency in weak interactions). Chen Ning Yang and Tsung-Dao Lee, theorists who had proposed the invalidity, were awarded the Nobel Prize in Physics; Wu's contribution was neglected.

β-decay: the emission of an electron in the transformation of a neutron into a proton.

Donald Mastick (103)

rarest earth: Elements in the lanthanum and actinide series of the periodic table, including plutonium, are known as "rare earth metals."

Wahl: As a doctoral student at the University of California, Berkeley, Arthur Wahl was part of a team that first isolated plutonium. He headed the Plutonium Chemistry Group at Los Alamos.

Hempelmann: Louis Hempelmann directed the Health Group at Los Alamos.

Oak Ridge: Hempelmann called Colonel Stafford Warren, medical director of the Manhattan Project (and later inventor of the mammogram), at his office in Oak Ridge—the site in Tennessee where uranium 235 was separated from the more abundant 238 isotope.

49: code name for plutonium 239, referring to the atomic number (94) and the mass number (239) of the isotope of plutonium used in the Nagasaki bomb.

Geiger-Müller: a Geiger counter.

lowly stock clerk: In March 1943, Mastick was the second scientist to arrive at Los Alamos. Initially, he worked setting up the supply of chemicals for Los Alamos; then he served on the laboratory's first planning board. Eventually he shifted to doing actual chemistry, as the laboratory began to receive samples of fissionable materials. After his accident, he transferred to Wendover Air Force Base in Utah, where the 509th Composite Group—the unit responsible for delivering nuclear weapons in combat—had set up an isolated headquarters. At Wendover, Mastick was in charge of ordering equipment and supplies as an administrative assistant to Commander Frederick Ashworth, who supervised testing of bomb components.

Louis Slotin (108)

twenty-five: code name for uranium 235, based on the atomic number (92) and the mass number (235) of the isotope of uranium used in the Hiroshima bomb.

Cy Smith: Cyril Stanley Smith, a British metallurgist, who led the Metallurgy Group at Los Alamos.

Hanford: Hanford, Washington, was the site of the Manhattan Project's plutonium production plant.

Kitty Oppenheimer (110)

Peter: Kitty and Robert's first child, nicknamed Pronto because he was born seven months after they were married.

A month alone in Reno: Kitty and Robert fell in love while she was still married to her third husband, Richard Harrison, a British doctor living in Los Angeles. In the autumn of 1940, she moved to Reno to get a quick divorce and then immediately married Robert.

Tyke: Kitty and Robert's second child, Katherine, aka Toni, was born at Los Alamos on December 7, 1944.

Joseph Rotblat (116)

Hitler's tanks: In early 1943, Colonel Benjamin "Monk" Dickson, head of G-2 for the American II Corps in Tunisia, predicted that the Nazis would attack through the Faid Pass in the eastern Atlas Mountains, and he requested British reinforcements—but the British First Army was fooled by Nazi diversions around Ousseltia and therefore concentrated their forces farther north, leading to a decisive defeat of the Allied forces.

John Dudley (118)

Luzon: The largest of the Philippine islands.

George Kistiakowsky (119)

Shangri-La: An ironic nickname for Los Alamos, referring to the paradisiacal valley in James Hilton's 1933 novel, *Lost Horizon*.

Jornada: Spanish for "workday," but more specifically referring to a measurement of distance based on how far one can travel in a day. Jornada del Muerto ("Workday [or Journey] of the Dead") was the name of the desert region in southern New Mexico that was chosen as the site of the Trinity test of the first plutonium bomb.

Dorothy McKibben (123)

Joe: McKibben's husband died of Hodgkin's lymphoma in 1931.

TB: McKibben first came to New Mexico in 1925 to recover from tuberculosis at the Sunmount Sanitarium in Santa Fe.

Norris Bradbury (125)

Source: This poem is based on a memo written by Bradbury, titled "TR Hot Run."

G-engineers: Marshall Holloway and *Philip Morrison*, members of *Otto Frisch*'s Critical Assembly Group, were assigned as the "Gadget engineers," responsible for overseeing acquisition or manufacture and then testing of all bomb core components contained within the HE shell.

HE: high explosive.

Jercinovic: Leo "Jerry" Jercinovic, a chemical engineer in the SED (Special Engineer Detachment), an army unit composed of men chosen for their technical backgrounds and assigned to Los Alamos, where they worked side by side with civilian scientists but earned less money, lived in army barracks, and were subject to military discipline. Jercinovic worked in the explosives group and rode with the HE assembly to the Trinity tower, where the fissionable core was inserted before the bomb was raised to the top of the tower.

Frank Oppenheimer (128)

LeMay: General Curtis LeMay was the Army Air Force officer in charge of strategic operations against Japan. In response to frequent cloud cover, strong winds, and the Japanese use of a cottage-industry approach to military manufacturing, he shifted from daylight high-altitude precision bombing to a program of nighttime firebombing of Japanese cities, which killed hundreds of thousands of Japanese civilians and destroyed dozens of cities.

Valle Grande: a grass valley in the Jemez Caldera in the mountains above Los Alamos.

Donald Hornig (131)

Kisty: *George Kistiakowsky*, leader of the Explosives Division at Los Alamos.

count the miles by fifths: Each second a thunderclap travels approximately ⅕ of a mile.

Leslie Groves (135)

Major General: Groves was promoted in December 1944.

a joke: By the time of the Trinity test, the fear that a nuclear weapon might ignite the atmosphere could be treated as a joke, but only because the theoretical scientists had studied the possibility seriously beforehand.

Littlefield: Sergeant Steward Littlefield.

Ike: General Dwight Eisenhower, Supreme Allied Commander in Europe.

Mac: General Douglas MacArthur, Supreme Allied Commander in the Southwest Pacific.

Hubbard: Jack Hubbard, chief meteorologist for the Trinity test.

Holzman: Colonel Benjamin Holzman, an Army Air Force meteorologist.

St. Supplice: Groves's misnomer for Saint-Sulpice-et-Cameyrac, the location of "a venereal camp" near the docks at Bassens, across the Garonne River from Bordeaux, which Groves visited in 1919 as a student on an inspection tour of Army Corps of Engineers projects in France.

Rayburn: Sam Rayburn, Speaker of the House during World War II.

Barkley: Alben Barkley, Senate Majority Leader during World War II.

Bridges: Styles Bridges, a powerful US Senator.

Schrafts: candies manufactured by the Boston-based Schrafft Candy Company, founded in 1861.

Mrs. O: Jean O'Leary was Groves's personal secretary.

Harvard's president: James Conant was a chemist, president of Harvard from 1933 to 1953, and chairman of the National Defense Research Committee, which oversaw the Manhattan Project, from 1941 to 1947. He lay on the ground beside Groves during the Trinity test.

Philip Morrison (138)

three SEDs: The Special Engineer Detachment was an army unit composed of men chosen for their technical backgrounds and assigned to Los Alamos.

Sam: Samuel Allison, an American physicist, was the Chemical Group leader and then the director of the Chicago Metallurgical Laboratory, a division of the Manhattan Project tasked with developing the first nuclear reactor and studying the chemistry and metallurgy of plutonium. In November 1944 he moved to Los Alamos as the Chair of the Technical and Scheduling Committee and a member, along with Robert Bacher and *George Kistiakowsky*, of the Cowpuncher Committee responsible for "riding herd" on the Trinity test.

Thomas Farrell (141)

Source: This poem is based on Farrell's "impressions," included in *Leslie Groves*'s "Memorandum for the Secretary of War" (July 18, 1945) reporting on the Trinity Test.

Victor Weisskopf (143)

Grünewald's altarpiece: The *Isenheim Altarpiece*, painted by Matthias Grünewald in 1512–1516 for the Monastery of St. Anthony in Isenheim, Alsace, and now housed in the Unterlinden Museum in nearby Colmar.

J. Robert Oppenheimer (144)

Vishnu: one of the three primary gods of Hinduism that represent the Trimurti— the three primary functions of the cosmos. Vishnu is the Preserver, Brahma the Creator, and Shiva the Destroyer. Vishnu is portrayed as having many arms. To teach the prince (Arjuna), he transforms into Shiva, the "Red God," associated with the sun.

Joan Hinton (145)

Oscura Mountains: a range to the east of the Trinity site.

David McDonald (146)

Source: David McDonald's poems are reworkings of his own words from interviews included in Jon Else's 1980 documentary, *The Day After Trinity*.

Hans Bethe (147)

Nothing like the sun: In his search for metaphors to comprehend his experience of the Trinity test, "Bethe" echoes a number of literary touchstones, among them Shakespeare's "Sonnet 130" and Hopkins's "The Windhover."

David Nicodemus (150)

Frisch: *Otto Frisch*, German physicist, Critical Assembly Group leader, and part of the British mission to Los Alamos.

our village: Nicodemus grew up in Sendai, Japan, the son of missionary teachers.

the men's school: the Tohoku Gakuin, where Nicodemus's father taught.

Mukoyama: Nicodemus's spelling of the Sendai ward now transliterated as "Mukaiyama"; site of the Daimanji Buddhist temple, across the Natori River from the men's school.

honey buckets: buckets used as portable toilets.

Hannya mask: a mask used in Noh theater, representing a woman transformed by jealousy into a devil.

a young marine biologist: the emperor Hirohito.

Hirose-gawa: the Hirose River, a tributary of the Natori River in Sendai.

"And he rebuked the winds": a conflation of various Biblical passages, e.g., Isaiah 11:15, Mark 4:39, Matthew 8:26.

a hillside thirty kliks away: Many of the scientists, such as *Edward Teller*, who were not involved in conducting the Trinity test, gathered on Compaña Hill to witness the results of their work.

Harriet "Petey" Peterson (153)

Smitty: Major Ralph Carlisle Smith, Patent Group leader at Los Alamos.

Drs. Love and Large and Stout: Selby Love was the Los Alamos base pediatrician, Alfred Large the chief surgeon, and James Stout the obstetrician.

Fat man or thin: The original gun-type plutonium weapon design was nicknamed "Thin Man"; it was superseded by the implosion design actually detonated over Nagasaki, known as "Fat Man." The line also refers to a distinct physiological contrast between Groves and Oppenheimer.

Joe Willis (155)

the *Chieftain*: *El Defensor Chieftain*, a newspaper based in Socorro, New Mexico, near the Trinity site, reported that "Miss Georgia Green," a blind girl, had seen the flash of the Trinity test; the story has been widely circulated ever since.

Els: Georgia's sister and Joe's wife.

Lucina: Georgia's mother.

Jean Vaissade: A popular French accordionist and composer, Vaissade was Edith Piaf's first coach and helped start Django Reinhardt's career.

the *Bunker Hill*: a US aircraft carrier struck by two kamikaze planes while supporting the invasion of Okinawa.

Kistler's: Kistler-Collister, a clothing store in Albuquerque.

Lemitar: a town northwest of the Trinity test site.

Peerless carbon arc: a Peerless Magnarc movie projector lamp manufactured by the J. E. McAuley Manufacturing Company of Chicago.

J. Robert Oppenheimer (161)

Source: This poem is based on one of Oppenheimer's own, published in June 1928 in *Hound and Horn*, a literary magazine founded by Harvard undergraduates.

Crisis: Oppenheimer's horse.

Sources

The characters who speak through these poems are all based on real people—some well-known historical figures, others obscure private citizens. In crafting verse voices for these individuals, I have tried to remain faithful to the historical record and, whenever possible, to their own writings and pronouncements, both published and unpublished. Indeed, in a few instances (the Norris Bradbury, Thomas Farrell, and David McDonald poems, along with the final J. Robert Oppenheimer), I have reworked existing sources; in other cases, I have invented voices based on only scraps and hints. At both poles, and in the latitudes between, for the past thirty-three years I have carefully surveyed the territory, visiting Manhattan Project sites, delving into archives, attending reunions of both military and scientific personnel, and interviewing and corresponding with project participants. In undertaking this work, my intent has been to offer the reader representations of historical truth.

And yet, though I have looked to these individuals to identify the events and actions that mattered most to them, to reveal their perspectives and insights as well as the phrases, images, and metaphors with which they responded to their experiences, the historical record contains both too little information and too much. For each voice I have had to choose which details to highlight and which to omit; I have interpreted, filled in gaps, and found analogues; arranged and juxtaposed; matched spoken to poetic rhythms; concentrated extensive webs of thought and feeling into moments of crisis; implied personality through syntax, lineation, and structure. And so the voices in these poems are indeed "characters" and not those people they are emblems of. This is, I hope, not a flaw but a feature, for there is also the truth of fiction.

To convey both kinds of "truth," I have turned to verse, hoping, through the juxtapositions of rhyme, the stutter step of enjambment, the metrical shadings of thought and feeling—all the time-tested techniques by which poetry voices a multiplicity of human meanings in every line—to capture something of the complex attitudes and beliefs these people clove to or betrayed; to tease apart the ways in which their proximity to nuclear weapons inspired revision of their personal narratives and metaphorical armatures; to understand how they normalized the unthinkable, how pacifists created weapons of mass destruction, how scientists left their ivory towers to work for the military, and how their attitudes and actions thrust us all, willy-nilly, into the nuclear age.

Why go to such lengths to produce mere poems? Something at the core of these people—something that made their participation in the Manhattan Project both possible and ultimately productive—is crucially important to the rest of us, not only because it enabled them to transform our world but because it inhabits us as well. Our future, as they framed and we enact it, depends on our understanding of that something, and poetry is particularly suited to the task, for, over the millennia, it has developed as a peculiar but effective medium through which to explore and extend the resources of language as a means of expressing, and shaping, the inner life of the individual. Poetry has evolved both to convey and to challenge convention, to engage ambiguity and to nurture nuance, to make music and to meditate on meaning, to hand down history and to reconceive the self. If we hope to move beyond propaganda, sound bites, and received wisdom, poetry is surely one of our best bets.

Not least among poetry's virtues is its difficulty. It requires that we wrestle with language, ideas, perceptions, experiences—our own and other people's—much as the individuals who inspired these poems did. Poetry resists simple conclusions; it undercuts static understanding; it engages individual effort. The result is that each of us will ultimately develop our own conceptions of the individuals portrayed here. For those readers who may be interested in pursuing these matters further, there is a voluminous "literature" about the Manhattan Project, by both participants and historians. The following list includes those sources I have found most useful that are also reasonably accessible.

Start With

Rhodes, Richard. *The Making of the Atomic Bomb*. New York: Simon and Schuster, 1986. Reprinted with a new foreword, 2012.

Else, Jon. *The Day After Trinity*. KTEH public television, 1980.

The Atomic Heritage Foundation. http://www.atomicheritage.org.

History and Background of the Manhattan Project

Boyer, Paul. *By the Bomb's Early Light: American Thought and Culture at the Dawn of the Atomic Age*. New York: Pantheon, 1985.

Church, Fermor, and Peggy Pond Church. *When Los Alamos was a Ranch School*. Los Alamos, NM: Los Alamos Historical Society, 1974.

Conant, Jennet. *109 East Palace: Robert Oppenheimer and the Secret City of Los Alamos*. New York: Simon and Schuster, 2005.

Davis, Nuel Pharr. *Lawrence & Oppenheimer*. New York: Simon and Schuster, 1968.

Goodchild, Peter. *J. Robert Oppenheimer: Shatterer of Worlds*. Boston: Houghton Mifflin, 1981.

Groueffe, Stephane. *Manhattan Project*. Boston: Little, Brown, 1967.

Hawkins, David. *Project Y: The Los Alamos Story*. Part 1, *Toward Trinity*. Los Angeles: Tomash, 1983.

Herken, Gregg. *Brotherhood of the Bomb: The Tangled Lives and Loyalties of Robert Oppenheimer, Ernest Lawrence, and Edward Teller*. New York: Henry Holt, 2002.

Hewlett, Richard, and Oscar Anderson. *The New World, 1939/1946*. Philadelphia: Pennsylvania State University Press, 1962.

Hoddeson, Lillian, Paul Henriksen, Roger Meade, and Catherine Westfall. *Critical Assembly: A Technical History of Los Alamos during the Oppenheimer Years, 1943–1945*. Cambridge, UK: Cambridge University Press, 1993.

Howes, Ruth H., and Caroline L. Herzenberg. *Their Day in the Sun: Women of the Manhattan Project*. Philadelphia: Temple University Press, 1999.

Hyde, Montgomery H. *The Atom Bomb Spies*. London: Sphere Books, 1980.

Jungk, Robert. *Brighter than a Thousand Suns*. New York: Penguin, 1958.

Knebel, Fletcher, and Charles Bailey. *No High Ground: The Secret History of the Hiroshima Bomb*. London: Weidenfeld and Nicolson, 1960.

Kunetka, James. *City of Fire*. Albuquerque: University of New Mexico Press, 1979.

Kurzman, Dan. *Day of the Bomb*. London: Widenfeld and Nicolson, 1986.

Lamont, Lansing. *Day of Trinity*. New York: Athaneum, 1965.

Pettit, Roland A. *Los Alamos before the Dawn*. Los Alamos, NM: Pajarito Publications, 1972.

Purcell, John. *The Best-Kept Secret: The Story of the Atomic Bomb*. New York: Vanguard, 1963.

Reid, R. W. *Tongues of Conscience: War and the Scientists' Dilemma*. London: Constable, 1969.

Smyth, Henry. *Atomic Energy for Military Purposes*. Washington, DC: US Government Printing Office, 1945.

Truslow, Edith. *Manhattan District History: Nonscientific Aspects of Los Alamos Project Y, 1942–1946*. Los Alamos, NM: Los Alamos Historical Society, 1991.

US Department of Energy. *Trinity Site*. Washington, DC: US Department of Energy, 1992.

Walker, Stephen. *Shockwave: Countdown to Hiroshima*. New York: HarperCollins, 2005.

Weart, Spencer. *The Rise of Nuclear Fear*. Cambridge, MA: Harvard University Press, 2012.

Wyden, Peter. *Day One: Before Hiroshima and After*. New York: Simon and Schuster, 1984.

Books by and about Manhattan Project Participants

Badash, Lawrence, Joseph Hirschfelder, and Herbert Broida, eds. *Reminiscences of Los Alamos, 1943–1945*. London: D. Reidel, 1980.

Barut, Asim O., Halis Odabasi, and Alwyn van der Merwe, eds. *Selected Popular Writing of E. U. Condon*. New York: Springer-Verlag, 1991.

Bernstein, Jeremy. *Oppenheimer: Portrait of an Enigma*. Chicago: Ivan R. Dee, 2004.

Bethe, Hans. *The Road from Los Alamos*. New York: Simon and Schuster, 1991.

Bird, Kai, and Martin Sherwin. *American Prometheus: The Triumph and Tragedy of J. Robert Oppenheimer*. New York: Alfred A. Knopf, 2005.

Brode, Bernice. *Tales of Los Alamos: Life on the Mesa, 1943–1945*. Los Alamos, NM: Los Alamos Historical Society, 1997.

Burns, Patrick, ed. *In the Shadow of Los Alamos: Selected Writings of Edith Warner*. Albuquerque: University of New Mexico Press, 2001.

Church, Peggy Pond. *The House at Otowi Bridge: The Story of Edith Warner and Los Alamos*. Albuquerque: University of New Mexico Press, 1960.

Clark, Ronald W. *Einstein: The Life and Times*. New York: World, 1971.

Fermi, Laura. *Atoms in the Family*. Chicago: University of Chicago Press, 1954.

Feynman, Michelle, ed. *Perfectly Reasonable Deviations from the Beaten Track: The Letters of Richard P. Feynman*. New York: Basic Books, 2005.

Feynman, Richard. *The Character of Physical Law*. Cambridge, MA: MIT Press, 1967.

Feynman, Richard, as told to Ralph Leighton. *Surely You're Joking, Mr. Feynman!* Edited by Edward Hutchings. New York: Norton, 1985.

———. *What Do You Care What Other People Think?* New York: Norton, 1988.

Fisher, Phyllis. *Los Alamos Experience*. New York: Japan Publications, 1985.

French, A. P., ed. *Einstein: A Centenary Volume*. Cambridge, MA: Harvard University Press, 1979.

French, A. P., and P. J. Kennedy, eds. *Niels Bohr: A Centenary Volume*. Cambridge, MA: Harvard University Press, 1985.

Frisch, Otto. *What Little I Remember*. Cambridge, UK: Cambridge University Press, 1979.

Gamow, George. *Thirty Years That Shook Physics*. New York: Dover, 1966.

Gleick, James. *Genius: The Life and Science of Richard Feynman*. New York: Vintage, 1992.

Groves, Leslie. *Now It Can Be Told*. New York: Harper, 1962.

Hull, McAllister, with Amy Bianco. *Rider of the Pale Horse: A Memoir of Los Alamos and Beyond*. Albuquerque: University of New Mexico Press, 2005.

Jette, Eleanor. *Inside Box 1662*. Los Alamos, NM: Los Alamos Historical Society, 1977.

Kunetka, James. *Oppenheimer: The Years of Risk*. Englewood Cliffs, NJ: Prentice Hall, 1982.

Lanouette, William. *Genius in the Shadows: A Biography of Leo Szilard, the Man Behind the Bomb*. Chicago: University of Chicago Press, 1992.

Larsen, Rebecca. *Oppenheimer and the Atomic Bomb*. New York: Franklin Watts, 1988.

Laurence, William. *Dawn Over Zero*. London: Museum Press, 1947.

———. *Men and Atoms*. New York: Simon and Schuster, 1959.

Lewis, Richard, and Jane Wilson, eds. *Alamogordo Plus Twenty-Five Years*. New York: Viking, 1970.

Libby, Leona Marshall. *The Uranium People*. New York: Crane Russak and Charles Scribner's Sons, 1979.

Masters, Dexter, and Katherine Way, eds. *One World or None*. London: Latimer House, 1947.

McMillan, Elsie Blumer. *The Atom and Eve*. New York: Vantage Press, 1995.

Mehra, Jagdish. *The Beat of a Different Drum: The Life and Science of Richard Feynman*. Oxford, UK: Oxford University Press, 1994.

Michelmore, Peter. *The Swift Years: The Robert Oppenheimer Story*. New York: Dodd Mead, 1969.

Monk, Ray. *Robert Oppenheimer: A Life Inside the Center*. New York: Doubleday, 2012.

Moore, Ruth. *Niels Bohr: The Man, His Science, and the World They Changed*. New York: Knopf, 1966.

Morrison, Philip. *Philip Morrison's Long Look at the Literature*. New York: W. H. Freeman, 1990.

Norris, Robert S. *Racing for the Bomb: General Leslie R. Groves, the Manhattan Project's Indispensable Man*. South Royalton, VT: Steerforth Press, 2002.

Numerof, Paul. *In August 1945*. Los Alamos, NM: Los Alamos Historical Society, 2006.

Oppenheimer, Robert. *Atom and Void: Essays on Science and Community*. Princeton, NJ: Princeton University Press, 1989.

———. *Letters and Recollections*. Edited by Alice Kimball Smith and Charles Weiner. Cambridge, MA: Harvard University Press, 1980.

———. *Science and the Common Understanding*. London: Oxford University Press, 1954.

———. *Uncommon Sense*. Boston: Birkhauser, 1984.

Pais, Abraham. *Niels Bohr's Times in Physics, Philosophy, and Polity*. Oxford, UK: Oxford University Press, 1991.

———. *"Subtle Is the Lord . . .": The Science and the Life of Albert Einstein*. Oxford, UK: Oxford University Press, 1982.

Peierls, Rudolph. *Bird of Passage*. Princeton: Princeton University Press, 1985.

Segrè, Emilio. *A Mind Always in Motion: The Autobiography of Emilio Segrè*. Berkeley: University of California Press, 1993.

Serber, Robert. *The Los Alamos Primer: The First Lectures on How to Build an Atomic Bomb*. Edited by Richard Rhodes. Berkeley: University of California Press, 1992.

Serbert, Robert, with Robert P. Crease. *Peace and War: Reminiscences of a Life on the Frontiers of Science*. New York: Columbia University Press, 1998.

Silva, Peer de. *Sub Rosa: The CIA and the Uses of Intelligence*. New York: Times Books, 1978.

Smith, Alice Kimball. *A Peril and a Hope: The Scientists' Movement in America, 1945–47*. Cambridge, MA: MIT Press, 1970.

Smith, Cyril Stanley. *A Search for Structure: Selected Essays on Science, Art, and History*. Cambridge, MA: MIT Press, 1981.

Sparks, Ralph C. *Twilight Time: A Soldier's Role in the Manhattan Project at Los Alamos*. Los Alamos, NM: Los Alamos Historical Society, 2000.

Steeper, Nancy Cook. *Dorothy Scarritt McKibbin: Gatekeeper to Los Alamos*. Los Alamos, NM: Los Alamos Historical Society, 2003.

Sykes, Christopher. *No Ordinary Genius: The Illustrated Richard Feynman*. New York: Norton, 1994.

Szasz, Ferenc Morton. *The Day the Sun Rose Twice: The Story of the Trinity Site Nuclear Explosion, July 16, 1945*. Albuquerque: University of New Mexico Press, 1984.

Szilard, Leo. *The Voice of the Dolphins and Other Stories*. New York: Simon and Schuster, 1961.

Teller, Edward. *The Legacy of Hiroshima*. New York: Doubleday, 1962.

———. *Memoirs: A Twentieth-Century Journey in Science and Politics.* Cambridge, MA: Perseus Publishing, 2001.

Ulam, Stanislaw. *Adventures of a Mathematician.* New York: Scribners, 1976.

Weart, Spencer, and Gertrud Weiss Szilard, eds. *Leo Szilard: His Version of the Facts.* Cambridge, MA: MIT Press, 1978.

Weaver, Warren. *The Scientists Speak.* New York: Boni & Gaer, 1947.

Weisskopf, Victor. *The Joy of Insight: Passions of a Physicist.* New York: Basic Books, 1991.

———. *Knowledge and Wonder: The Natural World as Man Knows It.* Rev. ed. Cambridge, MA: MIT Press, 1979.

———. *Physics in the Twentieth Century: Selected Essays.* Cambridge, MA: MIT Press, 1972.

———. *The Privilege of Being a Physicist.* New York: W. H. Freeman, 1989.

Wigner, Eugene, P., as told to Andrew Szanton. *The Recollections of Eugene P. Wigner.* New York: Plenum Press, 1992.

Wilson, Jane, ed. *All In Our Time.* Chicago: Bulletin of the Atomic Scientists, 1975.

Wilson, Jane, and Charlotte Serber, eds. *Standing By and Making Do: Women of Wartime Los Alamos.* Los Alamos, NM: Los Alamos Historical Society, 1988.

Biographical Notes

Hans Bethe, husband of Rose Bethe, led the Theoretical Division at Los Alamos. Before the war, he wrote the definitive account of energy production in stars.

Rose Bethe, daughter of German physicist Paul Ewald, was the wife of Nobel physicist Hans Bethe. At Robert Oppenheimer's request, Bethe preceded her husband to Los Alamos, where she headed the Housing Office.

Niels Bohr, one of the seminal figures in twentieth-century physics, founded the Institute of Theoretical Physics at the University of Copenhagen in 1920. Best known for developing an influential model of the atom and for the complementarity principle—the assertion that understanding natural phenomena requires application of mutually exclusive conceptual and measurement frameworks—he was equally important as a mentor to other physicists and as a resource for those fleeing Nazi persecution. In 1943 he was himself forced to flee, first to Britain in the bomb bay of an RAF Mosquito and then to the United States, where he served as a consultant to the Manhattan Project, contributing both technical and philosophical guidance.

Norris Bradbury oversaw assembly of the high-explosive charges that would detonate the plutonium bomb in the Trinity test. When Robert Oppenheimer resigned after the war, Bradbury took over as the scientific director of Los Alamos.

Bernice Brode came to Los Alamos with her husband, Bob, a physicist who developed the fuses for the Hiroshima and Nagasaki bombs, and their two sons, Bill and Jack. She was trained as a computer and helped calculate shock wave dynamics.

Appolonia Chalee grew up near Los Alamos and worked as a maid for the scientists' families during the war.

Janet Coatesworth was called to the King's Crown Hotel to take Leo Szilard's dictation of the letter Einstein would send to Franklin Roosevelt.

Edward Condon left his job as the director of the Westinghouse Research Laboratories to serve as Robert Oppenheimer's principal assistant when the Los Alamos lab opened in March of 1943. Though he was already at home in the New Mexican landscape (he had been born in Alamogordo, near the site that would eventually be chosen for the Trinity test), a variety of concerns—perhaps most importantly that military compartmentalization would doom the already iffy project—led Condon to resign after only six weeks. Before he left, he wrote up Robert Serber's lectures at the opening colloquium to serve as a "primer" for new arrivals at Los Alamos.

Max Delbrück began his career as a physicist in Copenhagen, where he knew Niels Bohr, and Berlin, where he worked for Lise Meitner. In 1937 he gave up physics and moved to Caltech to study genetics, the field in which he eventually won a Nobel Prize.

Peer de Silva mistrusted Robert Oppenheimer so intensely (and vociferously) that, to defuse his opposition, Groves appointed him head of military intelligence at Los Alamos, where he could personally keep an eye on Oppenheimer and the many "communists" Oppie recruited to work on the first atomic bombs. After the war, de Silva joined the nascent CIA, eventually serving as station chief in Vienna, Seoul, Hong Kong, Saigon, and Bangkok.

John Dudley was the Army Corps of Engineers officer charged with finding a location for the secret laboratory where the first atomic bombs would be designed and built. His choice, Jemez Springs, was rejected by Oppenheimer and Groves in favor of Los Alamos. At his request, he was later transferred to an engineer regiment in the Pacific Theater.

Albert Einstein signed a letter in August 1939 alerting President Franklin Roosevelt to the possibility that nuclear fission might be used to make "extremely powerful bombs of a new type" and that Nazi Germany was probably already working on them. At the time, Einstein was summering on Long Island, where he spent his time sailing and working on his "hobbyhorse," Unified Field Theory.

Thomas Farrell served with distinction in World War I. He retired from military life in 1926 but returned to active service in the Army Corps of Engineers ten months before the United States entered World War II. In 1944, Henry Stimson, the secretary of war, concerned that Leslie Groves had become indispensable, directed Groves to choose a "Number Two man": "You can have any officer in the Army, no matter who he is, or what duty he is on." Groves's first choice was Farrell.

Richard Feynman was the youngest group leader at Los Alamos. His wife, Arline, lived in a tuberculosis sanatorium in Albuquerque during most of Feynman's time on "the Hill." As her tuberculosis worsened, she and Feynman sent each other puzzles and codes. This annoyed the censors but helped Arline pass the time between Feynman's visits. She died in 1945, shortly before the Trinity test.

Otto Frisch, along with his aunt, Lise Meitner, interpreted, in December 1938, Otto Hahn and Fritz Strassmann's analysis of experimental results produced by Meitner, Hahn, and Strassmann in their work on radium, and, in the process, Frisch and Meitner "discovered" (and named) nuclear fission. Frisch later joined the British bomb project and was part of the contingent that moved to Los Alamos to support the Manhattan Project.

Klaus Fuchs grew up in Germany. His sister Elisabeth was killed when she jumped in front of a train to escape arrest for communist activities, and his brother, Gerhard, was imprisoned, also for his communist affiliations. Their mother committed suicide by drinking hydrochloric acid. Fuchs fled to England with his sister Christel to escape persecution for his own Communist Party connections. He was initially sent to a detention camp in Canada but was soon allowed to return to England, where he joined the British atomic bomb project as a physicist. During this time he began sharing details of his work with the Soviet government. In 1944, he traveled with Frisch and the rest of the British mission to Los Alamos, where he continued his work as a physicist and a spy.

Leslie Groves was a colonel in the Army Corps of Engineers when he was named head of the Manhattan Project in September 1942. Groves resisted the assignment, thinking the bomb project was almost certain to fail and claiming he had his hopes set on combat duty. He eventually accepted the job, on the condition that he be made brigadier general, and then pushed the project with relentless energy.

Willy Higinbotham, a young engineer from MIT, was appointed head of the Electronics Group. He was beloved for, among other things, his skill on the accordion, which he played at dances and during movie intermissions.

Joan Hinton joined the Los Alamos laboratory while still a physics graduate student at the University of Wisconsin. She worked under Enrico Fermi, building low- and high-powered enriched uranium reactors. After the war she moved to China where she and her husband ran a dairy farm outside Beijing.

Donald Hornig earned his PhD in chemistry for his work on explosives. At Los Alamos he designed the spark gap switch at the heart of the X unit that triggered the Fat Man bomb. During the night leading up to the Trinity Test, Groves and Oppenheimer worried that someone might try to sabotage the implosion bomb. Hornig was assigned to sit with the bomb at the top of the test tower as a thunderstorm lit up the surrounding desert.

George Kistiakowsky, "the number one civilian explosives expert" during the war, took over leadership of implosion experimentation from Seth Neddermeyer, whose formal scientific approach was too plodding. "Kisty" introduced techniques for creating explosive lenses, instituted controversial safety protocols, and relied on hundreds of young, untried technicians to construct and test his innovative castings, even resorting to borrowing an electric dentist's drill to remove unwanted air bubbles. He left to ferry the high-explosive implosion assembly to Trinity at a few minutes past midnight on Friday, July 13, 1945.

John Lansdale Jr. graduated from the Virginia Military Institute and Harvard Law School and joined the Army Reserve. He was called to active duty in G-2 (military intelligence) in 1941, and his responsibilities soon became focused on the fledgling efforts to build nuclear weapons. From June of 1942 on, he served as head of security and intelligence gathering for the Manhattan Project.

William Laurence, a reporter for the *New York Times* and the only member of the press permitted to witness the Trinity test, wrote the press releases that provided the background for every news story, worldwide, following the bombing of Hiroshima on August 6, 1945.

Ruth Marshak accompanied her husband, physicist Robert Marshak, to Los Alamos. Like many of the scientists' spouses, she was not privy to the purpose of the work being done there.

Antonio Martinez (Tewa name: Popovi Da), son of the famous potter Maria Martinez, grew up in the San Ildefonso Pueblo near Los Alamos. During the war, he was drafted into the army and assigned to work as a technical assistant at Los Alamos.

Donald Mastick worked with Arthur Wahl, one of the discoverers of plutonium, conducting ultra microchemical studies of the first tiny samples of the new element as they arrived from the Hanford piles. On August 1, 1944, a vial burst, coating Mastick's mouth with plutonium solution. Louis Hempelmann, the doctor in charge of radiation safety, pumped the contents of Mastick's stomach into a beaker, then handed it to Mastick to retrieve the plutonium. Shortly afterward, Mastick requested a transfer to the 509th Composite Group at Wendover Air Force Base, where he worked as an assistant to Commander Fred Ashworth, ordering equipment and supplies in preparation for dropping the atomic bombs on Japan.

David McDonald owned a ranch in southern New Mexico. It was commandeered by the air force for use as a bombing range and was ultimately chosen as the site for the Trinity test in July 1945.

Dorothy McKibben's ability to liaise between the Los Alamos laboratory and the Santa Fe community, fulfilling the needs and indulging the whims of a multitude of scientists and their families while keeping the project's purpose secret (it took her a year to figure out the lab's mission herself), earned her nicknames ranging from Gatekeeper of Los Alamos to Mother Superior. She first came to Santa Fe in 1925 to recover from tuberculosis and then moved there permanently with her two-year-old son, Kevin, after her husband, Joe, died of Hodgkin's lymphoma in 1931. Between them, she and Oppenheimer provided the two halves of a spiritual compass for the "Lost Almosts."

Philip Morrison studied under Oppenheimer at Berkeley, earning his PhD in physics in 1940. At Los Alamos he led a group in the Theoretical Division. After the Trinity test, he served as a physicist at the air force base on Tinian, assisting in the preparations for the atomic bombings of Japan. He visited Hiroshima shortly after the war ended as part of a scientific research group gathering data on the effects of nuclear weapons.

David Nicodemus was born in Kobe, Japan, and grew up in Sendai, where his parents were Presbyterian missionaries. March winds made fires common and difficult to fight, and in 1919 most of the city burned, including the missionaries' school. At Los Alamos, Nicodemus was a member of the RaLa committee that used radioactive lanthanum to measure the implosion shock waves used to trigger the plutonium bomb.

James Nolan served both military and civilian personnel at Los Alamos as an army physician, specializing in obstetrics and gynecology. He was obliged to combat an outbreak of the clap among a group of women and the bachelor scientists whose "basic needs" they had been "requiting."

Frank Oppenheimer, eight years younger than his brother Robert, worked on the separation of uranium isotopes in Berkeley and Oak Ridge until May of 1945, when he was transferred to Los Alamos to help with preparations for the Trinity test.

J. Robert Oppenheimer held dual teaching positions in theoretical physics at Caltech and Berkeley before Leslie Groves appointed him scientific director of the Los Alamos Laboratory. Given Oppenheimer's lack of either administrative experience or the cachet of a Nobel Prize, and in the face of his acknowledged leftist politics, it was "a most improbable appointment," as even his friend, Isidor Rabi, had to admit; yet it turned out to be "a real stroke of genius on the part of General Groves, who was not generally considered to be a genius." Oppenheimer stepped into the role as though born to it, succeeding beyond all expectation and fulfilling a wish he had expressed years before when he wrote to a friend, "My two great loves are physics and desert country. It's a pity they can't be combined."

Kitty Oppenheimer was Robert's first wife; he her fourth husband. She first married a jazz musician while a student at the Sorbonne, but his drug addiction led to an annulment. She then married a communist organizer from Ohio; he was killed in the Spanish Civil War. While studying for a degree in biology at the University of Pennsylvania, she married a British doctor and they moved to Pasadena where she met Robert. In May of 1941, Kitty gave birth to her first child, Peter, nicknamed Pronto because he arrived seven months after she married Robert. Although she didn't care for motherhood, like many of the wives at Los Alamos she found herself pregnant again in the spring of 1944. She gave birth to their second child, a daughter named Katherine (nicknamed Tyke and, later, Toni) on the third anniversary of the Japanese attack on Pearl Harbor.

Harriet "Petey" Peterson worked as a nurse at the Los Alamos hospital. After the war, she married Major Ralph Carlisle "Smitty" Smith, the head of the Los Alamos patent office.

Joseph Rotblat, a Polish physicist, was a member of the British mission to Los Alamos. After the defeat of Germany, he was the only senior scientist to leave the project. In 1957, he and Bertrand Russell founded the Pugwash Conferences on Science and World Affairs, of which he served as secretary-general for many years. He was awarded the Nobel Peace Prize (jointly with the Pugwash Conferences) in 1995.

Alexander Sachs was an economist and investment banker as well as a friend and advisor to Franklin Roosevelt. In October 1939 he hand-delivered (and read out loud) Einstein's famous letter to Roosevelt urging a liaison between the federal government and scientists working on the possibility of using nuclear fission as a source of energy and weaponry.

Robert Serber studied and taught under Robert Oppenheimer at Berkeley before joining the Manhattan Project as a theoretical physicist. In March 1943, he delivered a series of lectures, later mimeographed and nicknamed the Los Alamos Primer, to bring incoming scientists "up to speed" on the bomb project. He led the Diffusion Theory Group at Los Alamos and later worked at the air force base on Tinian, preparing for the bombings of Hiroshima and Nagasaki. Immediately after the war, he visited Japan as part of a scientific team gathering data on the effects of nuclear weapons.

Louis Slotin, a Canadian physicist, had little luck finding an academic job after receiving his PhD. He worked for a couple of years as a lab assistant before transferring to Los Alamos, where he ran critical mass experiments nicknamed Tickling the Dragon's Tail. He was killed by radiation in a lab accident in May 1946.

Leo Szilard, a Hungarian physicist, recognized the possibility of a nuclear chain reaction and patented the idea (in the name of the British Admiralty) in 1936. He drafted, and convinced Einstein to sign, the letter that initiated the US government's interest in nuclear weapons.

Edward Teller is best known as "the father of the hydrogen bomb." At Los Alamos, he led the Super and General Theory Group in F Division, which focused on topics other than the project's main task of designing a workable fission bomb. In particular, Teller was already intent on developing his ideas for a fusion "Super" bomb. Wigner nicknamed Teller, Szilard, and himself Martians when all three Hungarians were young physicists in Berlin. As a student in Munich, Teller lost his right foot in a tram accident.

Edith Warner moved from Philadelphia to New Mexico before the war, seeking a place to recover from tuberculosis. To support herself, she established a teahouse by the Rio Grande, near Los Alamos, where she lived with an older Native American man named Tilano. During the war, she served scientists from the mesa exclusively, making them long, leisurely dinners and providing a secure location in which they could relax and escape for a few hours from the pressures of their work.

Victor Weisskopf, an Austrian physicist, served as leader of the Efficiency Theory Group in the Theoretical Division at Los Alamos.

Eugene Wigner (nicknamed Wigwam) worked as a physicist for the Manhattan Project in its Princeton, Oak Ridge, and Chicago divisions. He drove his friend and fellow Hungarian Leo Szilard to Long Island during the summer of 1939 to meet with Einstein and discuss how best to alert world leaders to the threat of a Nazi nuclear weapon. He won a Nobel Prize in Physics in 1963.

Joe Willis lived with his wife, Els; her sister Georgia; and their mother, Abbie Lucina, in Socorro, near the Trinity test site. Georgia was born with a deformed eye, which was removed when she was three years old; a few years later, she damaged her remaining eye and from that time was largely though not entirely blind. On the morning of the Trinity test, Joe and Els were driving Georgia to Albuquerque, where she was a student at the university. When the flash from the bomb test lit up the horizon behind them, Georgia noticed the sudden light and asked, "What was that?" A local newspaper later made a fuss over the fact that a "blind" girl had apparently "seen" the Trinity burst. Since then this miraculous event has been cited as evidence of the bomb's mystical power.

Chien-Shiung Wu was a Manhattan Project physicist in Hanford, Washington, where uranium breeder reactors were used to produce plutonium. Her experimental work confirmed the theoretical arguments of two colleagues on the invalidity of the principle of conservation of parity. Her colleagues were awarded a Nobel Prize in Physics, for which Wu was overlooked.